Texas Family Law for
School Administrators, Teachers, and Lawyers

Texas Family Law for School Administrators, Teachers, and Lawyers

Wading through Divorce and Custody Issues on Your Campus and in Your School District

SECOND EDITION

Kevin Lungwitz and Jeana Lungwitz
Attorneys, The Lungwitz Law Firm, P.C.

Park Place Publications
Austin, Texas

First edition published 2010. Second edition 2012.

512 W Martin Luther King Jr Blvd, #300
Austin, TX 78701
(512) 478-2113 • Fax: (512) 495-9955
www.ed311.com

First Printing: June 2012
Second Printing: August 2014
Third Printing: October 2015
Fourth Printing: September 2016

ISBN 978-0-9833083-3-1

Contents

Introduction

Have you ever been in a meeting with parents of a student at your school when the parents disagree with each other? They both look to you and other school staff with the expectation that you will break the tie and agree in favor of one of them or the other. You try to avoid eye contact with either of them as you look at the ceiling and grasp for just the right diplomatic words, but you find yourself talking in circles and trying to kill time, even though you know that rarely solves the issue. You struggle to find a solution that will leave them both happy, but you know in your heart that appeasement never works and will leave them both angry.

So who gets to make the educational decisions at hand when the parents disagree? Mom? Dad? You? The counselor? The nurse? Perhaps a law should be passed authorizing the assistant principal to handle such issues and to impose a binding, nonappealable solution. That would certainly provide fertile training ground for all aspiring administrators and would test the mettle of a candidate for principal. The last time we checked, no such bill was pending in the legislature.

Maybe the situation described above would be an easy one for you. Maybe you *wish* there was a mom and a dad who would actually come to school and sit in a shared meeting regarding their child and that the conflict could fairly be characterized as only a "disagreement." It could certainly be worse, or at least more complicated to figure out.

Feuding parents, separated parents, divorced parents, abusive parents, stepparents, grandparents, same-sex parents, Mom's new boyfriend or girlfriend, Dad's new girlfriend or boyfriend, other guardians, adult siblings—all looking to you to settle educational issues (and potential legal issues) regarding their child, or at least a child they lay claim to. And remember, you and your administrative team are responsible for keeping students, parents/guardians, your staff, the community, your supervisors, and the school board all happy—at the same time. Such is the life of a mid-level manager.

Not to worry. You are not alone.

There is safety and strength in numbers. All school employees face difficult situations when dealing with children and their families. Teachers and administrators are often unfairly put in the middle of emotionally charged family law struggles while attempting to accomplish their primary goal of educating children. The purpose of this book is to provide guidance to school administrators, teachers, and other school employees when these circumstances arise. It will no doubt provide guidance to school attorneys as well. We sincerely hope that you will find this resource helpful in this regard.

The original edition of this book was written in 2009 and 2010 and published in 2010. Since then, there have been legislative changes, which we have noted in this revised edition. Also, we have made some stylistic changes upon reflection after delivering numerous legal trainings on the book. We hope this revised edition is even easier to read and understand than the first.

We have arranged the book in such a way as to provide you with a quick compendium of useful terms when dealing with family law at school, with brief chapters on a variety of family law issues. Many hypothetical situations are posed and tackled in an attempt to make this a beneficial and practical administrative guide rather than an academic treatise.

The topics addressed are the culmination of questions asked at several Texas school seminars where we provided training on the topic "Do I Have to Get between Mom and Dad? Family Law for the School Administrator." It is our goal with this book to demystify Texas family law in easy-to-digest portions for busy school administrators and teachers, as well as lawyers.

This is a *Texas* book. Family law and school law are matters largely left to the states. Therefore school laws and family laws can and do vary between the states. Also, as with any legal guide, *nothing in this book is intended as legal advice.* At the risk of sounding too lawyerly, this is actually an ironclad rule. Legal cases are almost always fact-driven and can turn on the slightest factual nuance, of which there may be many. Legal advice in such matters is best dispensed discreetly between administrators, teachers, supervisors, and the school's lawyer. If you sense that legal trouble is brewing in your school, you should seek clearance from your supervisors to discuss the matter with the school's lawyer.

None of these legal caveats should stand in the way of your deeper understanding of Texas family law in the schools, however. If that is what you are seeking, then this book is for you.

Texas Family Law for
School Administrators, Teachers, and Lawyers

Chapter 1

Terminology in Court Orders

Legal jargon can be strange. We can only imagine the frustration when a nonlawyer attempts to read a court document or legal treatise written by a lawyer who seemingly gets paid by the word. Rest assured, there are many who share that frustration. We think the language used in some legal documents can be confusing, vague, and cryptic—and we've been to law school! Family law has its fair share of special terms, but the list of terms you may encounter in a family law court order is finite. These terms, most of which are set forth below, are easily mastered with some practice and study.

Reading a Court Order

Half of being a lawyer is reading things other people don't want to. Often it doesn't take any particular skill—just dogged persistence to finish. Reading a family court order falls into this category. You can learn a lot by merely reading the document. Although Texas court orders seem long and tedious, they set out rather specifically the rights and duties of parents to the child. Historically, the orders were very brief and vague. Due to litigation through the years, orders continue to grow longer, but have become more specific—longer to read, but in the end, perhaps easier to understand.

Easy rule: *If any controversy or disagreement arises regarding parental rights over a child at your school, you should read the court order provided by a parent* (if such an order exists). Court orders should contain the answers to the vast majority of your school-related, family law questions.

Custody

One word that arises in a discussion of family law is "custody." It certainly sounds like a legitimate family law term. You may hear about a "custody suit," or someone may refer to a "custody order." Oddly enough, the word "custody" can be found nowhere in Texas family law statutes. When the term "custody" is bantered about in family law, it is really referring to one or more of the following three issues:

I. Conservatorship: Who has the right to make certain **decisions** about the child?
II. Possession and access: Who has the right to **physical possession** of the child, and when?
III. Child support? Who has the duty to **financially support** the child, and how much?

Every family law court order involving children will contain provisions addressing these three critical areas and, in doing so, will address what most people commonly refer to as "custody."

Following are some terms typically found in court orders regarding children:

I. Conservatorship: Who Has the Right to Make Certain Decisions about the Child?

"Conservatorship" is a broad term to describe a person who has the right to make certain decisions concerning a child. You've probably heard of "joint managing conservators," "sole managing conservators," and maybe even "possessory conservators." These types of conservators will be described later. But as you will come to learn, it is far less important to know what kind of conservator a parent is (joint, sole, or possessory) than to learn what rights the court has given the parent.

"Conservatorship" is a term that comes up only in the context of a legal proceeding concerning the child. In other words, if there has been no lawsuit regarding the child, there will be no one named a conservator. Conservatorship of a child has nothing to do with who has the right to physical possession of a child; it simply deals with who has certain decision-making authority for the child.

There is usually more than one conservator of a child—typically each parent is a conservator. In this book we routinely and casually refer to conservators as parents. This keeps it simple. However, despite a presumption in Texas law that the parents will be named conservators of a child, there are situations when a parent may not be named a conservator. The following situations are some examples:

- If a parent has not had contact with the child in a very long time
- If a parent has a severe substance abuse issue
- If a parent is expected to be incarcerated for a long time
- If a parent is a danger to the child
- If a parent has a remarkable mental impairment
- If a parent's rights have been terminated (usually either voluntarily or due to abuse or neglect—see "Termination of Parental Rights," below)

In cases where a parent is not named as a conservator, there might be a long list of characters who could fill this role and with whom you might be interacting at your school: grandparents, aunts, uncles, or any other adult deemed worthy by the court to fulfill such a role.

As we have established, conservatorship is about decision making. The Texas Family Code divides the decision-making rights over a child into three categories:

A. Decision-making rights at all times (without regard to whether the parent is in possession of the child at that particular moment)
B. Decision-making rights that occur only during periods of possession of the child
C. What we affectionately call, for lack of a better phrase, the "Big Rights," which include the right to make educational decisions

A. Rights at All Times

All conservators, regardless of whether they are

joint managing, sole managing, or possessory, typically have the following rights *at all times,* regardless of whether the child is currently in their possession. (Education-related rights are in bold.)

1. **The right to receive information from the other parent and to confer with the other parent in making decisions concerning the** health, **education**, and welfare **of the child**
2. **The right of access to the** medical, dental, psychological, and **educational records of the child**
3. The right to consult with a physician, dentist, or psychologist of the child
4. **The right to consult with school officials concerning the child's educational status and school activities**
5. **The right to attend school activities**
6. **The right to be designated on a child's records as a person to be notified in case of emergency**
7. The right to consent to medical, dental, and surgical treatment during an emergency involving an immediate danger to the health and safety of the child
8. The right to manage the estate of the child to the extent the estate has been created by the parent or the parent's family[1]

B. Rights during Periods of Possession of the Child

All conservators typically have the following rights *only during their periods of possession* of the child. (There are no education-related rights here.)

1. The duty of care, control, protection, and reasonable discipline of the child
2. The duty to support the child including providing the child with clothing, food, shelter, and medical and dental care not involving an invasive procedure
3. The right to consent for the child to medical and dental care not involving an invasive procedure
4. The right to direct the moral and religious training of the child[2]

C. The Big Rights

The "Big Rights" are the rights that make divorce lawyers rich. Divorces and custody battles are often vigorously fought over the control of these rights because they relate to the ultimate care issues regarding a child. (The most substantial education-related right is in bold.)

1. The right to establish the primary residence of the child
2. The right to consent to medical, dental, and surgical treatment involving invasive procedures
3. The right to consent to psychiatric and psychological treatment
4. The right to receive and give receipt for periodic payments for the support of the child and to hold or disburse these funds for the benefit of the child
5. The right to represent the child in legal action and to make other decisions of substantial legal significance concerning the child
6. The right to consent to marriage and to enlistment in the armed forces of the United States
7. **The right to make decisions**

concerning the child's education

8. The right to the services and earnings of the child
9. Except when a guardian of the child's estate or a guardian or attorney ad litem has been appointed for the child, the right to act as an agent of the child in relation to the child's estate if the child's action is required by a state, the United States, or a foreign government[3]

Did you catch that? Big Right number 7 is "the right to make decisions concerning the child's education." Most conservators will share the rather mundane rights to confer with the other parent, teachers, and school officials regarding school matters, to receive school-related information, to attend school activities, and to be notified in an emergency, but "the right to make decisions concerning the child's education" is very special for our purposes. The parent with this right gets to call the school-related shots. You need to find out which parent/conservator has this right. If this right is shared by the parents (and we hope for your sake it is not), your job could become more challenging. What if they disagree? More on that later.

Rights at all times . . . Rights during possession . . . The Big Rights . . . Joint managing, sole managing, and possessory conservators . . . How do you keep all of this straight?

Easy rule: *A parent has only the rights attributed to that parent in the court order.* Said another way, if a right is not listed in the court order, the parent does not have that right. Said yet another way, a court order is not likely to affirmatively state that a parent does *not* have a right; rather, it will simply be omitted from that parent's list of rights. It doesn't matter what the right is or what kind of conservator the parent is. If the right isn't listed, the parent doesn't have it.

D. Joint Managing Conservator

There is a presumption in Texas law that both parents will be named joint managing conservators. It presumably advances the public policy of this state to at least make it *sound* as if both parents are equally engaged in the raising of their children. But this term may be confusing and even misleading. "Joint managing conservators" sounds like two parents who have equal, or "joint," decision-making authority for a child, but this is not always the case. In some joint managing conservatorships, one parent might have all of the Big Rights, and the other parent might not have any. Again, the type of conservator is not important—rather, what's important is the list of rights attributed to the parent that are specified in the order.

You may, however, encounter a "true" joint managing conservatorship, which reflects the court's genuine attempt to create a power-sharing arrangement between two parents. In such cases, the Big Rights are awarded to the parents in one of three ways:

- They are divided up between the parents (e.g., one parent may have the right to make invasive medical decisions, while another parent has the right to make educational decisions).

- The conservators may be required to make decisions together regarding the child (e.g., the parents may be required to agree on educational decisions for the child). As intimated above, this arrangement is not preferred, because it may create a dilemma for school officials should the parents disagree. But no one asked us and no one asked you—so we will have to figure out how to deal with this (see chapter 3).

Or

- Each conservator may have the right to independently make decisions regarding the child. Like the second scenario listed immediately above, this arrangement will not work well for educational purposes if the parents are not in agreement. For example, what if each parent having the right to make educational decisions enrolls the child in a different school?

It should never be assumed that parents have equal decision-making power concerning children, despite what they are called in the order. The court order itself will delineate which parent has the right to make which decisions, at what time, concerning the child. Parents who are splitting up tend to be in emotional turmoil. This can cause them to get very attached to titles. Many lawsuits are settled by calling a parent a "joint managing conservator" even though that parent is not given the rights of a "joint managing conservator." The rights of each parent will be spelled out in the order. It is worth noting again that a parent has only the traditional rights attributed to that parent in the court order. If a right is omitted, a parent does not have that right.

E. Sole Managing Conservator

In some cases, instead of parents being named joint managing conservators, one parent is named a sole managing conservator and the other is named a possessory conservator. A sole managing conservator is usually the person who exclusively holds all of the Big Rights. Both parents will typically have the "rights at all times" and the "rights during periods of possession." Usually when one person is named the sole managing conservator, another person will be named the possessory conservator.

F. Possessory Conservator

Don't be deceived by the name. A possessory conservator typically will have the "rights at all times" and the "rights during periods of possession" but will almost never have any of the Big Rights. This term may be confusing because it sounds like the possessory conservator would have possession of the child most of the time. This isn't so. Recall that conservatorships deal with decision-making authority regarding a child, not with physical possession of the child. Yet it stands to reason that since a possessory conservator has much less decision-making authority regarding a child, the possessory conservator will usually wind up with the lesser amount of physical possession of the child.

II. Possession and Access: Who Has the Right to Physical Possession of the Child, and When?

The part of the order pertaining to possession and access sets out when the child is going to be with Mom, Dad, or a grandmother or aunt, and so forth, as the case may be. Most court orders provide that the conservators shall have the child as agreed to, and failing mutual agreement, the child will be with each parent as set out in the very specific terms in the order. Why is this important to you? Because this is the part of the order that defines when each parent is entitled to possession of the child in question. For example, this will help you settle an argument about who is entitled to pick up the child next Thursday.

A standard possession order (also known as an SPO) provides that the parents will have possession of the child whenever they mutually agree.[4] If a child is at least three years old, there is a presumption in Texas that, at a minimum, a parent who does not have primary possession of the child will have possession of the child according to a specific schedule set out in a statute.[5] Of course there are exceptions to this general rule, so the order must be read to determine exactly the schedule the family is operating under. What happens if the parents cannot agree? The order will set out the specific schedule. It will state that the parent who does not have primary possession will have the child at the following times:

- *Weekends*—Beginning at 6:00 p.m. on the first, third, and fifth Fridays of the month and ending the following Sunday evening at 6:00 p.m. Some orders will provide that the visit will begin when school is out on Friday, and end when school resumes on Monday. If there is a holiday on Friday when the visitation begins or on Monday when the visitation ends, the visitation will begin a day earlier or end a day later, as applicable. If the conservators live over 100 miles apart, instead of the first, third, and fifth weekend, the visiting conservator may choose to visit one weekend per month of his or her choice by giving the other conservator 14 days' notice.
- *Thursdays*—Every Thursday evening during the school year from 6:00 to 8:00 p.m. In some orders this day may be Wednesday or some other day of the week.
- *Spring break*—The conservators will alternate who has the child during spring break if they live within 100 miles of each other. If they live more than 100 miles from each other, the visiting conservator will have the child every spring break.
- *Summer*—If the conservators live within 100 miles of each other, the visiting conservator will have the child for 30 days in the summer, during which the primary conservator can have one weekend. If the conservators live more than 100 miles from each other, the visiting conservator will have the child for 42 days in the summer during which the primary conservator may choose up to two weekends to have possession of the child. Further, the primary conservator may designate up to 21 days of continuous possession of the child during the summer months.
- *Thanksgiving*—The parents will alternate who has the child for the Thanksgiving holiday. The Thanksgiving holiday begins at 6:00 p.m. on the date that school lets out and ends at 6:00 p.m. on the day before school resumes after the Thanksgiving break. Of course many orders will provide that the holiday will begin when school lets out, and end when school resumes.
- *Christmas break*—One conservator will have the child from 6 p.m. on the day school lets out for the winter break until noon

on December 28. The other conservator will have the child beginning at noon on December 28 until 6:00 p.m. on the day before school resumes. This schedule will alternate each year.

- *Child's birthday*—The conservator who does not have the child with him/her on the child's birthday will have the child from 6:00 p.m. to 8:00 p.m. on that day.
- *Mother's Day and Father's Day*—Assuming the conservators are parents of the child, the mother will have the child with her for Mother's Day Weekend, and the father will have the child with him for Father's Day Weekend.[6]

Again, the order will set out the schedule specifically. Many orders will be set out in the terms above, but some situations require orders that are more customized (e.g., no overnight visits; dates or times of visitation changed due to the work schedules of the conservators; periods of visitation required to be supervised by another adult; etc.).

III. Child Support: Who Has the Duty to Financially Support the Child, and How Much?

Who has to pay how much to support the child can be an emotional part of a family law case. Lucky for you, this is rarely of any concern for school officials. While it is certainly conceivable that you may have a personal opinion about child support in a particular case on your campus, child support issues should be of little concern to you as a professional matter.

Other Important Terms in Court Orders

Suit Affecting the Parent-Child Relationship

More commonly known as a "custody suit," a suit affecting the parent-child relationship (abbreviated by lawyers as SAPCR, pronounced SAP-SIR) is a lawsuit filed to settle issues of conservatorship, possession and access, and child support.

Best Interest of the Child

The court must determine that all of the provisions in the custody order are in the best interest of the child. Of course, reasonable minds may differ on this point. Whatever the fact finder (judge or jury) determines is in the child's best interest is what matters in these sorts of lawsuits.[7]

Protective Order

A protective order can be issued by a court when someone has been violent or has threatened to be violent with another person.[8] To obtain a protective order, the parties must have a certain sort of relationship (be related by blood or marriage, or former spouses, or dating, or live in the same household, etc.). A protective order will typically order the person who has been violent to stay a certain distance away from the school, home, and employment of a person protected by the order (a "stay away" provision), among other things. Unlike most civil court orders, protective orders are criminally enforceable. For example, if an order says that Dad is prohibited from coming within 200 yards of child's school, and Dad shows up at the school, law enforcement can be called and Dad can be arrested. Another unusual feature of a protective order is that the parties cannot agree to ignore a "stay away" provision. Only a court can change this part of the order. So if there is a protective order that says Dad cannot come within 200 yards of the school, and Mom calls to say that it is fine for Dad to come to the school to pick up the child, it is not. Mom and Dad cannot agree to change this term of the order—only the judge can. Protective orders are valid for the length of time stated in the order. If there is no expiration date on the order, Texas law provides that it expires two years after the date it was issued.[9] If the person restricted by the order is incarcerated on the date the order expires, the order is valid until one year after the release from incarceration.[10]

Temporary Restraining Order

Temporary restraining orders are typical in cases where parties have filed a custody suit or filed for divorce. The purpose of the temporary restraining order is to keep the status quo until the parties can get to court and have a judge decide what the rules are going to be while a case is pending.[11] These orders are typically requested by one party to the suit before the other party to the suit has been notified that a suit has been filed. Standard provisions of a temporary restraining order include that a parent will not disturb the peace of a child or take a child out of a certain geographical area until a hearing is held. After a temporary restraining order is obtained, there will usually be a hearing within a couple of weeks, at which a court will determine some temporary rules (called temporary orders) that will be operative until a final order is in place.

Temporary Orders

Temporary orders set out the rules that parties are going to live by until a final order is made in a custody or divorce suit. Unlike the temporary restraining order that is issued prior to one of the parties to a suit being notified that a suit has been filed, temporary orders are issued by a court after everyone has been given notice and a hearing has been held. Temporary orders are important because they can address the very heart of a divorce and custody case. Although temporary, these orders may be in place for quite some time until the underlying lawsuit is resolved, and they may be given weight by the judge in the final resolution of the case. Temporary orders may determine issues of conservatorship, possession and access, and child support.

Temporary orders are not always requested, and so they may not exist. In some cases temporary orders are not needed because the parties are in agreement and do not need the assistance of a judge. In other cases, the parties need temporary orders but cannot afford the cost of this extra step. Thus, not every divorce and custody case will include temporary orders. It certainly benefits school employees when parents seek temporary orders. These orders tell you who has the authority to make education-related decisions with respect to the child while the underlying custody suit is pending. If the custody suit takes months or years to resolve, and if the parents are very disagreeable during this time, this could cause you prolonged administrative heartburn. You may find yourself strongly encouraging the parents to seek temporary orders if they are continuously placing you in the middle of their struggles involving their child.

Termination of Parental Rights

There are two situations in which a biological or adoptive parent of a child may no longer have legal rights to the child:

- Voluntary termination—This occurs when a parent voluntarily gives up his or her rights to a child by signing a statement relinquishing those rights, and later a judge signs an order declaring that the individual is no longer the parent of that child.[12]
- Involuntary termination—This may occur in cases of abuse and/or neglect. A court may determine that a parent is no longer legally allowed to be a parent to the child, and may involuntarily terminate a parent's rights.[13]

Whether voluntary or involuntary, if a parent's rights to a child are terminated, it makes the parent a legal stranger to the child.[14] The former parent has no rights to see the child or make any decisions about the child, nor does he or she have any obligation to pay child support.

Guardian

A guardian is someone who has been deemed by a court to be the legal caretaker of another person in instances where the person is unable to take care of himself or herself. In most instances where families are whole, there will be no need for a guardian, because a parent or parents will be named as conservators. A guardian is typically named for a child when the child's parents are deceased or the parents' rights have been terminated by a court. The guardian may or may not be related to the child. Unless a person can produce a court order showing that he or she is the guardian of a child, that person is not the legal guardian of the child.[15]

Power of Attorney

An adult may sign a document allowing another adult to exercise certain rights on his or her behalf.[16] This document is not a court order and will not be signed by a judge. It is called a power of attorney. The document will state what rights an individual is allowing someone else to exercise, and will state specifically who the individual is allowing to exercise those rights on his or her behalf. For example, a parent may sign a power of attorney allowing a grandparent to make educational decisions for a child. So long as the parent has these rights (i.e., the parent's rights to make educational decisions have not been limited by a court order), this delegation of powers is legitimate. Signing a power of attorney does not limit the parent's ability to make these decisions, but it does add another person who may make these decisions. The person signing the power of attorney may revoke the document at any time. Some powers of attorney will have an expiration date written on the document. See chapter 4 for further discussion about powers of attorney, and see chapter 6 for examples.

Chapter 2

Who Is a Parent?

Only parents have the right to make decisions on behalf of a child unless there is a court order to the contrary. This sounds like an easy concept, and thankfully, it usually is. However, in the context of schools and education, the lines separating those who may invoke parental authority over a child and those who may not can become blurred. If you are coasting along fabulously in all of the family law issues on your campus, or at least no one has questioned "who is a parent," then consider yourself fortunate and skip the rest of this chapter. Unless there are persons at your school battling over *who is entitled to exercise parental authority,* or who stands in "parental relation," then you can move along—there is nothing more to see here. It will only cause your stomach to churn.

If, however, there are disputed issues as to who has parental authority over a certain student on your campus, then this chapter may shed some light on this issue. Complicating this issue is that there are several statutes that define "parent," and no two of them define it exactly the same way. So bear with us as we forge our way through this. Let's begin with the basics.

Definitions of "Parent" in State and Federal Statutes

Texas Family Code

The Texas Family Code defines a parent as a mother or father of the child.[1] More specifically, it defines a "mother" as one of the following:

1. The woman who gave birth to the child
2. A woman found by a court to be the mother of the child
3. A woman who adopted the child[2]

The definition of "father" is a bit more involved. A father is one of the following:

1. A man who is presumed to be the father of the child. In order for a man to be presumed to be the father of the child, one of the following things must be true:
    a. He married the mother of the child, and the child was born during the marriage.
    b. He was married to the mother of the child and the child was born before the 301st day after the date the marriage was terminated by death, annulment, declaration of invalidity, or divorce.

c. He married the mother of the child after the child was born, voluntarily said he was the father of the child, and either filed an assertion of his paternity with the bureau of vital statistics, or voluntarily put his name on the child's birth certificate, or promised in a record to support the child as his own.
d. He continuously lived with the child during the first two years of the child's life and represented to others that the child was his.

2. A man who has filed an acknowledgment of paternity that has not been rescinded or successfully challenged
3. A man whom a court has found to be the father of the child
4. A man who has adopted the child
5. A man who has consented to assisted reproduction by his wife, which resulted in the birth of the child (i.e., a surrogate situation)[3]

Easy rule: *Unless modified or altered by a court order, the definition of "parent" will always include at least a natural (biological) or adoptive parent.*

Texas Education Code

The Texas Education Code seems to embrace the definitions in the family code set out above, but it also seems to expand the definition of "parent" in a significant way. It says that "'parent' *includes a person standing in parental relation.*"[4] The term "parental relation" is a little vague, to put it lightly. One would think that surely this term has been nailed down in Texas jurisprudence so that honest school administrators will know with whom to conduct school business and that surely there is a court in this great state that has considered what it means to stand "in parental relation." Unfortunately, it hasn't and there isn't.[5]

To better frame this dilemma, consider this possible situation:

> *Scenario:* You have a *very* active stepdad of a model student on your campus. Stepdad is the PTA president, the Little League coach of the year, a scoutmaster, and he gives after-school cello lessons to the entire fourth grade. He has been raising his stepson for many years, providing all of the essential care for this child, and has done everything we would expect from an engaged parent—except that he has never adopted his stepson. He is a stepdad.
>
> The biological dad is still in the picture. Bio-dad and stepdad show up for the same meeting concerning the student. Bio-dad tells you (the principal) that Stepdad is not to be in this meeting, because he is not a parent. Stepdad looks at you, makes the peace sign, brings his fingers to his eyes and then in the direction of your eyes, and says, "But I stand in *parental relation* to my stepson, so I get full parental rights under the Texas Education Code." There is no court order, and Bio-dad has not had his parental rights modified.

How do you solve this problem? What are Bio-dad's rights? What are Stepdad's rights?

Short answer: Absent a court order to the contrary, Stepdad does *not* stand in parental relation and is *not* entitled to parental authority under the Texas Education Code.

Longer answer: Because there is no case law defining "a person standing in parental relation," this is a gray area. While the answer may seem a tad counterintuitive, since in this example Stepdad is Superstepfather, here is how this conclusion is reached: The term "in parental relation" was most likely intended to come into play *only when there is no biological or adoptive parent in the picture.* Otherwise a stepparent would have the same rights as a natural or adoptive parent, and this does not jibe with the flow and spirit of Texas family law.

Keep in mind that all issues regarding "who is a parent" will arise *only if a natural or adoptive parent raises them.* So when we say that a stepparent, grandparent, or other person has fewer rights than a natural or adoptive parent who is "in the picture," this is what we mean. If there isn't a natural or adoptive parent in the picture, who is going to object? With few exceptions, the school needs to be able to communicate with an adult on behalf of every child.[6] If there is no biological or adoptive parent in the picture, then you may accept another person who convincingly holds himself or herself out to be the primary caregiver of the student, as "a person standing in parental relation." When this occurs, the person who stands in parental relation acts in the place of, or instead of, a biological or adoptive parent and properly assumes parental authority over the student.

The Texas Education Code says that a school board "by policy may allow a person showing evidence of legal responsibility for a child other than an order of a court to substitute for a guardian or other person having lawful control of the child under an order of a court."[7] So a person believing that he or she has legal responsibility for a child may petition the school board or administration through the grievance process or some other method. Such an individual would have to show that he or she has legal responsibility for the child and seeks substitution for another person who has rights under a court order. Frankly, we are not sure what it means to have "legal responsibility" for a child if one is not a parent or already has some authority under a court order. This law is confusing, and there are no cases on point.

Two categories of people who are *not* parents in the context of education are (1) a person whose parental rights have been terminated by a court and (2) a person who is not entitled to possession of or access to (visitation with) a child.[8] (See chapter 4 for more on this topic.)

Easy rule: *For educational purposes, a parent is never someone whose parental rights have been terminated by a court or who is not entitled to possession of or access to a child.*

Individuals with Disabilities Education Act

Federal law has its own opinions of who a parent is. The Individuals with Disabilities Education Act (IDEA) defines a parent as one of the following:

A. A natural, adoptive, or foster parent of a child (unless a foster parent is prohibited by state law from serving as a parent)
B. A guardian (but not the state if the child is a ward of the state)
C. *An individual acting in the place of a natural or adoptive parent (including a grandparent, stepparent, or other relative)* with whom the child lives, or an individual who is legally responsible for the child's welfare
D. An individual assigned to be a surrogate parent[9]

Consider the Stepdad scenario again. What if the meeting in the same scenario above was an Admission, Review, and Dismissal (ARD) Committee meeting related to the child's disability and the IDEA therefore governs? What if Stepdad was temporarily representing Bio-mom, who could not attend? Does Stepdad get to stay? Isn't Stepdad ostensibly "an individual acting in the place of a natural parent with whom the child lives," according to the IDEA definition? Can Bio-dad have Stepdad thrown out of the meeting?

For the same reasons as stated above, absent a court order to the contrary, we side with Bio-dad: Stepdad must go. Since it is an ARD Committee meeting, then presumably the IDEA definition of "parent" would apply. If the IDEA definition is applied and Bio-mom cannot attend the meeting, Stepdad might argue that he gets to attend the meeting because he is acting "in the place of a natural parent"—that is, in place of Bio-mom. Bio-dad might argue that Stepdad doesn't get to be there because he, Bio-dad—"a natural parent"—is present, so there is no need for anyone to act in the place of a parent at the meeting. Again, we agree with Bio-dad.

If this is an issue on your campus, do these three things: (1) postpone the meeting, (2) encourage the parents to get a court order clarifying the issue, and (3) seek the guidance of the school attorney.

Not-So-Easy Rule: *Absent a court order or other controlling legal document, if there is a natural or adoptive parent in the picture, no other person is entitled to exercise parental rights*—not even a stepparent or grandparent. Check with your school lawyer.

Family Educational Rights and Privacy Act

The Family Educational Rights and Privacy Act (FERPA), the federal law governing access to student educational records, also defines parent a little differently. It says a parent is "a natural parent, a guardian, or an individual acting as a parent in the absence of a parent or a guardian."[10]

• • •

So we see that the Texas Education Code uses the term "standing in parental relation," IDEA uses the phrase "in the place of a natural or adoptive parent," and FERPA says that a parent includes "an individual acting as a parent in the absence of a parent or a guardian." We construe all of these terms to be synonymous with the common legal term *in loco parentis.* We used to think this was

Spanish for "crazy parent," but educators at an in-service workshop set us straight. *In loco parentis* is Latin for "in the place of a parent."

Indeed, Texas educators are granted limited, temporary, quasi-parental rights over students, because educators stand *in loco parentis* to students during the school day.[11] Lucky for you, these rights are available only in the absence of a parent. Once a parent appears on the scene, an educator no longer stands *in loco parentis* to a student. That right magically vanishes.

This is similar to the stepdad scenario above. If a natural or adoptive parent is not in the picture, another person may "stand in parental relation" or may act "in the place of a parent" or "in the absence of a parent." If a natural or adoptive parent *is* in the picture, no other person (not even a stepparent or a grandparent) has parental rights, absent a court order or other legal document.

Legal Documents That Confer Certain Rights to Nonparents

1. A **power of attorney** is a written instrument that allows a parent to convey his or her rights regarding a child, to another person.

2. An **authorization agreement for nonparent relative** allows a parent to sign an agreement with *a grandparent, an adult sibling, or an adult aunt or uncle of the child* that authorizes that person to perform certain acts in regard to the child. The education-related rights the parent can authorize to be exercised by the relative are enrolling the child in a public or private primary or secondary school and authorizing the child to participate in age-appropriate extracurricular activities, including athletic activities.[12]

These two instruments can certainly give you more "parents" or persons standing in parental relation with whom to deal in the school setting. These two instruments are explained and addressed in chapter 4.

Example Scenarios

Some example scenarios may be helpful as we hike through this rough terrain.

Scenario: Johnny has resided with Grandma for four and a half years, in the absence of any parent. Johnny does not live with Grandma for the sole purpose of attending your school. You have never met Mom or Dad and don't believe them to be in the picture. The grandmother enrolls Johnny in school. Grandma has no legal document saying she has custody of Johnny. Can the school refuse to enroll Johnny?

Answer: Probably not. In this example, Grandma is a person "standing in parental relation" to Johnny, since there is no natural or adoptive parent in the picture, so the school should interact with Grandma just as it would with a parent.[13] In addition, Johnny probably independently meets residency requirements under Texas school law. Also, the Texas Education Code allows a grandparent to enroll a child under some circumstances.[14]

• • •

Scenario: There are no court orders in place. Mom voluntarily leaves Johnny with Grandma. Mom lives out of town. Grandma enrolls Johnny in school. Dad comes to the school to withdraw Johnny in order to enroll him in the school district where Dad lives. Can Dad withdraw Johnny from school?

Answer: Yes. Dad's rights are superior to Grandma's unless the grandmother has a court order giving her superior rights to Dad's. Dad may withdraw Johnny from the school where the grandmother enrolled him.[15]

• • •

Scenario: There are no court orders in place. Mom voluntarily leaves Johnny with the grandmother (Mee-Maw). Mom lives out of town. Mee-Maw enrolls Johnny in the Gusher Independent School District, where Mee-Maw lives. Dad comes to the school to withdraw Johnny in order to enroll him in Dry Hole ISD, the school district where Dad lives. Mom shows up at the same time and demands that Johnny remain enrolled in Gusher ISD. Who has the right to decide where Johnny will be enrolled?

Answer: Unless there is a court order specifying which parent has the right to make educational decisions (usually a divorce decree or a custody order), then both parents have equal rights to make this decision.[16] However, Dad's rights should trump Mee-Maw's rights to enroll Johnny in Mee-Maw's place of residence. If the parents won't agree to settle this in your office with a round of Rock-Paper-Scissors, you should encourage them to get a court order in place specifying who has the right to make these decisions; and talk to the school attorney about what to do in the meantime.

• • •

Scenario: There are no court orders in place. Mom voluntarily leaves Johnny with her father (Pee-Paw). Mom lives out of town, and Pee-Paw enrolls Johnny in Tumbleweed ISD, where Pee-Paw lives. Dad's same-sex partner (SSP) comes to the school to withdraw Johnny in order to enroll him in Piney Woods ISD, the school district where Dad lives. Can the SSP withdraw Johnny from school?

Answer: Probably not. Assuming that Johnny primarily lives with Pee-Paw, Pee-Paw would most likely be seen as the person standing in parental relation to Johnny before the SSP. In this scenario, unless there is a court order to the contrary, Dad would have superior rights to Pee-Paw, but Pee-Paw would have superior rights to the SSP. The fact that there is a same-sex partner is irrelevant. Whether married to Dad or not, the SSP is like a stepparent. If Johnny primarily lives with Dad or spends equal time with Dad and Pee-Paw, then there might be no need to consider Pee-Paw as "standing in parental relation," because there is a parent in the picture. In this circumstance, the best practice would be to contact Dad and ask him to come take care of the withdrawal paperwork, since without a court order to the contrary he clearly has a superior right to both the SSP and Pee-Paw.

Easy rule: *Same-sex partners, stepparents, and others will have parental rights if they have adopted the child in question. Otherwise, they need some other legal document demonstrating their authority. If there is no biological or adoptive parent in the picture, then you may construe the person to stand in parental relation.*

Scenario: There is a court order stating that Mom has the right to make educational decisions for Cindy Lou Who. Mom is arrested and placed in jail. She executes a valid power of attorney allowing her mother (Gramma) to attend the ARD Committee meeting and make decisions about her child. Dad shows up and objects to Gramma's attendance and her assertion that she can make decisions for the child. Can Dad trump Gramma?

Answer: In this instance, Dad probably cannot trump Gramma, since the court order gives Mom the right to make educational decisions, and Mom has voluntarily given that right to Grandmother.

• • •

Scenario: The only adult you have ever dealt with is Gramps. You do not know about Mom or Dad. Gramps wants to review Little Bessie's special education records. Can he?

Answer: With no parent in the picture, it sure seems like Gramps stands in parental relation and is a person acting in the absence of a parent. If so, he can review the records and make decisions.

• • •

Scenario: Same as above, except that Mom shows up out of the blue and complains to you about Gramps. Gramps tells you that Mom's parental rights have been terminated, and he produces a court order. What do you do?

Answer: We stick with Gramps on this one. Assuming the court order is valid, Mom has no legal authority whatsoever toward the child. It is as if she is a legal stranger to the child. Gramps continues to "stand in parental relation."

Chapter 3

What Are the Basic Parental Rights in Education?

In chapter 2 we determined who a parent is, with respect to a child's education. In this chapter, we look at what the rights of parents are in relation to their children's education. Parents have many rights in public education. This chapter focuses on the rights parents have *when there is no court order limiting those rights.* Keep in mind that a court order can substantially limit parental rights. Also, a parent's bad behavior can limit those rights. However, absent a court order or bad behavior, all parents enjoy substantial rights pertaining to their children's education.

Parents as Partners in Education

In 1995 the Texas Education Code was given an extreme makeover that included the introduction of a whole chapter dedicated to parental rights. Chapter 26 of the code begins by saying: "Parents are partners with educators, administrators, and school district boards of trustees in their children's education. Parents shall be encouraged to actively participate in creating and implementing educational programs for their children."

Federal law mirrors this. Pursuant to the Elementary and Secondary Education Act (otherwise known as No Child Left Behind, or NCLB), every school district that is a recipient of Title I funds must have a written parent involvement policy that is developed with and approved by parents. The policy must describe how parents will assist the district in developing its Title I plan, and it must help parents know how to be included in educational decision making.

Further, the NCLB defines the term "parental involvement" as the participation of parents in regular, two-way, meaningful communication involving student academic learning and other school activities, including ensuring the following:

- That parents play an integral role in assisting their child's learning
- That parents are encouraged to be actively involved in their child's education at school
- That parents are full partners in their child's education and are included, as appropriate, in decision making and on advisory committees to assist in the education of their child[1]

Parent-Teacher Groups

A school board is required by law to cooperate in the establishment of at least one parent-teacher group at each school in the district, in order to promote parental involvement in school activities.[2] This further pushes a school district to open itself to parents.

Student Records

The Texas Education Code, the Texas Family Code, the federal Family Educational Rights and Privacy Act (FERPA), the Individuals with Disabilities Education Act (IDEA), and the Texas Public Information Act (TPIA) all guarantee parents the right to access and see student records pertaining to their child. (See chapter 7 for more discussion on student records.)

Easy rule: *Parents are always entitled to see their minor children's educational records, with only a few exceptions.*

Class Placement

Class placement is a subject of interest to parents, especially at the beginning of the school year—or during the year if things are not going well. Can a parent demand that his or her child be moved from Ms. Taylor's class to Ms. Lopez' class? The law gives a parent the right to "reasonable access to the school principal, or to a designated administrator with the authority to reassign a student, *to request a change in the class or teacher to which the parent's child has been assigned,* if the reassignment or change would not affect the assignment or reassignment of another student."[3]

The way this is worded makes it seem that such a request shall not be unreasonably denied, as long as it will not affect the assignment of another student.

Other Parental Rights

A parent may also reasonably request that his or her child be allowed to add an academic class (if economically practical), to attend a higher grade level (if the school official believes the child could succeed), and to graduate early (assuming the child has completed the requirements).[4] These are not absolute rights—because the school board has the final say[5]—but they are notable rights nonetheless.

Other extraneous parental rights are also found in the Texas Education Code:

- The right to review all teaching materials, textbooks, and other teaching aids used in the child's classroom and to review every test given to the child, including a state assessment test, after it is given. The school shall not unreasonably deny a parent's request for the child to bring home any textbook used in the classroom, provided the child will return the textbook the next day if the teacher makes that request.[6]
- The right to consent in writing before a school employee may make or authorize the making of a videotape of a child or record or authorize the recording of a child's voice.[7]
- The right to receive notice if the child is taught by an "inappropriately certified or uncertified teacher" for more than 30 consecutive days.[8]
- The right to temporarily remove a child from a class or activity because of a religious or moral conflict, if the parent delivers to the teacher a written statement authorizing the student's removal. This cannot be done to avoid a test or to avoid a class for an entire semester, however.[9]
- The right to access full information concerning a student, including information regarding special education.[10]
- The right to refuse psychiatric or psychological treatment of the child

without this becoming the sole basis for a child abuse or neglect report.[11]

- The right to access public school board meetings.[12]
- The right to file complaints with the school board and to be represented by an attorney in such complaints.[13]

Finally, the Texas Family Code sets out a list of rights and duties parents have, so long as they are not limited by a court order.[14] The education-related rights and duties listed are as follows:

- The right to make decisions regarding the child's education.[15]
- The duty to support the child, including providing the child with an education.[16]

The federal IDEA gives parents the right to be intimately involved in the identification and evaluation of a child's disability and the placement of the child into a special education program and to provide input into the child's individualized education plan (IEP), as well as other procedural protections.[17]

Open Communication with Parents

When a student's health, safety, or welfare at school or at a school event is an issue, or if the student is involved in anything strange or out of the ordinary, it is almost always a good idea for school officials to communicate with the parents as soon as possible. So often, it seems that parents are motivated to seek legal action against school officials when the parents believe that school officials have been less than forthcoming in communications or that school officials have delayed or otherwise failed in communicating. In one case, for example, an older student apparently sexually assaulted a younger student on a school bus. Although the bus driver reported it as soon as she returned to the bus barn, school officials did not notify the parents for another week. It is a general rule that school officials are not liable for injuries perpetrated by one student onto another student. However, a failure to inform the parents of such an incident and a failure to take action to protect an injured student from further harm can certainly fuel the parents' litigation and lead to potential liability for school officials.[18]

Parents Behaving Badly

While these lists of parental rights are not intended to be exhaustive, this point remains: Federal and state law intends and allows that parents be partners with educators in their children's education. These laws invest parents with substantial rights and control over their children's education. No doubt, educators could use more parental support, so that more education and less discipline might occur in school. However, what about the overbearing or abusive parent? Do these laws give parents the right to run the school? Do the partnerships envisioned in law extend all the way into the classroom? Not necessarily. Consider this example:

> *Scenario:* Mom drops off Little Precious with the first grade teacher every morning, and then stays. And stays. And stays. Mom has begun to impose herself on the class, interrupting and disagreeing with the teacher in front of the class. The teacher complains to you (the school principal) and requests that you tell Mom to leave. Can you tell Mom to leave? Isn't she a "partner" in her child's education under state and federal law?

Answer: You can tell this parent to leave and not return to the classroom. The partnership between parents and schools does not necessarily apply to the classroom. No person has a right to disrupt the educational environment. If Mom does not obey your verbal request, you may call the appropriate authorities to have her removed.

Easy rule: *No law or court ruling gives parents the right of uncontrolled access to the classroom or the right to disrupt the educational environment.* Despite the laudable overtures to parents in state and federal law, laws and court rulings give administrators wide latitude to secure a peaceful campus environment that is conducive to learning.

Case in point: Dad sued a Texas school district for allegedly limiting his access to his son at school. The restrictions put in place by the school were for good reasons. The court record reflected that Dad had yelled at his son's first grade teacher, swatted his child in front of the class, used profanity with school administrators, and harassed the teacher in the parking lot. Dad was ultimately told to refrain from communicating with teachers and to instead make appointments with the administration. He ignored this request and was eventually completely barred from the campus by the campus administration (with the assistance of the school lawyers). Still, he continued to taunt teachers. The police removed him from the campus on two occasions. The district court denied him any relief in his lawsuit, holding:

> [N]o court has ever interpreted the due process clause to create a parental right of unfettered access to school facilities. To the contrary, courts have consistently upheld the authority of school officials to control activities on school property. This includes barring third parties, including parents, from access to the premises when necessary to maintain order and prevent disruptions to the educational environment.[19]

It is actually a crime (Class C misdemeanor) to disrupt a classroom. Disruptions include (but are not limited to) entering a classroom without the consent of either the principal or the teacher and, through acts of misconduct or the use of loud or profane language, disrupting class activities.[20] It is also a crime (Class B misdemeanor) to engage in disruptive activities on school property or at a school event. However, let us be clear: A parent need not commit a crime before you ask the parent to change his or her behavior or before you ask the parent to leave the campus.

There are many laws and dynamics involving campus security and an administrator's right to enforce these laws for the sake of the school and the students. It is not the purpose of this chapter or this book to fully discuss campus security. We only seek to provide some clarity of the point that parental rights, like any other rights that exist in our society, are subject to being forfeited due to bad behavior and by the court system. While parents enjoy the broad right to be involved in education, this right is not an absolute.

As is shown, parents behaving badly stand in a position to forfeit some of their rights by administrative edict, even before a court gets involved. If you as an administrator reasonably believe that you must restrict a parent in some manner in order to provide a safe school environment, you may do so. It is always advisable to communicate these concerns to your supervisor and to the school lawyer so that you may receive proper assistance, because any action in this regard is likely to be challenged.

This chapter gives us a pretty good picture of the significant rights that parents have in the educational setting, so long as the parents do not behave badly, and assuming the family courts have not limited the parent's rights. Read on to the next chapter for more information about the ways in which parental rights may be modified by the courts.

Chapter 4

How Can Parental Rights Be Modified, Limited, Transferred, or Taken Away by a Court or a Legal Document?

As discussed in chapter 3, Texas and federal law gives parents many rights regarding their children's education. Specifically, Texas *family* law gives parents a long list of rights and duties regarding their children and their children's education.[1] Among these are the all-encompassing duties to provide the child with an education and the right to make decisions about the child's education.[2] However, like many rights in our society, these rights may be modified, limited, or removed under certain circumstances. A parent's rights may be limited by a court or transferred to a third party. Further, as discussed in chapter 2, the Texas Education Code expands the definition of "parent" to include someone "standing in parental relation" with the child.[3] In those instances, there are circumstances in which someone other than a parent will have the right to make educational decisions for a child.

In this chapter, we will address six instances where parental rights may be modified, limited, transferred, or taken away:

1. The termination of parental rights
2. A suit affecting the parent-child relationship
3. A protective order
4. Guardianship
5. A power of attorney
6. An authorization agreement for nonparent relative.

1. Termination of Parental Rights

Obviously, the right to make educational decisions for a child, as found in the Texas Family Code, is the greatest educational right of all. Yet a court order may limit a parent's rights related to a child, including the right to make educational decisions. This may happen in one of two ways. The *less common* way is when a parent's rights to his or her child have been completely taken away. This terminates not only the right to make educational decisions for the child but also every other parental right. The termination of parental rights may occur voluntarily, when a parent gives up all legal rights to the child; or a court may terminate a parent's rights involuntarily, due to child abuse or neglect.[4] Once a parent's rights are terminated, it is as if that parent is no longer the parent of the child. A parent whose rights have been terminated, whether voluntarily or involuntarily, does not have any rights to make any sort of decisions for that child, nor does that parent have any right to access the child.[5] For an example of a court order terminating parental rights, see appendix A.

Easy rule: *You do not have to deal with any person whose parental rights have been terminated.* The person is no longer a legal parent of the child. The person has no right to meet with teachers, see educational records, or attend school-related meetings regarding the child.

2. Suit Affecting the Parent-Child Relationship (SAPCR)

The second, *more common* circumstance whereby a parent's rights are affected by a court is through an order that modifies and limits the parent's rights but does not terminate them. This is typically seen in a custody suit, more formally known as a suit affecting the parent-child relationship (or SAPCR, pronounced SAP-SIR in the legal community); through a protective order (PO, pronounced PEE-OH by everyone); or through a guardianship proceeding.

First, we will talk about the SAPCR. If the parents are *married,* the SAPCR will be part of the divorce proceeding. People outside of the family law arena will commonly refer to this as a divorce and custody suit. If the parents are *not married,* the SAPCR will be its own lawsuit and will sometimes be commonly referred to as a custody suit.

Easy rule: *When parents are married, a SAPCR might be commonly referred to as a divorce and custody suit. When parents are not married, a SAPCR will be commonly referred to as simply a custody suit.*

In chapter 1, we discussed the three parts of a custody order:

- Conservatorship: Who has the right to make certain **decisions** about the child?
- Possession and access: Who has the right to **physical possession** of the child, and when?
- Child support: Who has the duty to **financially support** the child, and how much?

In this chapter, we are going to focus on conservatorship—*who has the right to make certain decisions about the child.* The conservatorship part of the order will tell you how the parents' rights have been limited or modified.

It's All About Conservatorship

Take a look at appendix B, an example of a final decree of divorce. Beginning on the third page of the order, you will notice that the parents are named Joint Managing Conservators.[6] Because of their titles, it sounds like both parents have equal rights—but take a closer look. Even in joint managing conservatorships, the parents will often have different rights. The title does not matter—what matters is the rights granted to each parent under each of the three parts of conservatorship rights. As you may recall from chapter 1, conservatorship is all about decision-making authority. Specifically, under what circumstances does which parent get to make certain decisions regarding the child? There are three parts to conservatorship:

A. Decision-making rights at all times (without regard to whether the parent is in possession of the child at that particular moment)

B. Decision-making rights that occur only during periods of possession of the child
C. What we affectionately call, for lack of a better phrase, the "Big Rights," which include the right to make educational decisions

The parents' rights in each of these areas will be specifically spelled out in the court order. In every court order where parents share some or all of the rights to the children, you will actually see the conservatorship part of the order divided into these three parts. Keep in mind that "Big Rights" is merely our descriptor—you won't see these rights called that in an order. In any event, these are the three sections you will want to focus on when confirming which parent has what rights to make certain decisions.

In the example order, both parents have the right to the child's school records (pages 3–4 of the decree in appendix B), but only Mom has the right to make educational decisions on behalf of the child and to attend school activities (page 3 of the order). Note that the order does not affirmatively deprive Dad of the right to make

> **Easy rule:** *A parent has only the rights attributed to that parent in the court order.* Said another way, *if a right is not listed in the court order, the parent does not have that right.* Said yet another way, a court order is not likely to affirmatively deprive a parent of a right; rather, the right will simply be omitted from that parent's list of rights. It doesn't matter what the right is or what kind of conservator the parent is. If the right isn't listed, the parent doesn't have it.

educational decisions or attend school activities, but those rights are omitted from his list of rights (page 4 of the order). If a right is omitted from the list, the parent does not have that right.[7] Dad does have the right to confer with Mom before she makes those decisions, but the school does not have to investigate whether this conference between the parents occurred.

Therefore, Dad does not have the right to make educational decisions or attend school activities, even though he has all of the following rights (page 3 of the order):

- To receive information from the other parent regarding the education of the child
- To confer with the other parent to the extent possible before decisions are made concerning the education of the child
- To access educational records of the child
- To consult with school officials concerning the child's education via phone or written communication

What About the Injunction Barring the Father from the School?

Please note that in the example divorce decree there is a permanent injunction issued prohibiting Father from going within 200 yards of the school, except as otherwise set out in the court order (pages 35–36 of the decree in appendix B). Most SAPCR orders will not contain permanent injunctions, but in cases with a high degree of acrimony, courts may issue them. When they do exist, permanent injunctions are typically found toward the end of the order, as this one is.

An injunction such as this is a civil mechanism that is not criminally enforceable. The mother owns this injunction, and only she can enforce it through a motion for contempt or other judicial action. However, the injunction in this example directly pertains to the school. What should you do if you know Dad is violating this injunction by going within 200 yards of the school? This can be a tricky question to answer, with many scenarios possible (e.g., you call Mom, and she does not mind that Dad has lunch with the child; Dad is behaving and is enjoying the school play with Mom; or Mom does not want Dad to be present, and/or Dad is being disruptive). To keep it from being so tricky, you should err on the side of protecting the school community.

Even though you don't want to create a scene when there isn't one, if the school is covered in the injunction, you should carefully take action. Depending on your safety and the safety of others, you should ask the father to leave, or summon law enforcement to have that discussion with the father. If the mother disagrees with this, she can go back to court and have the injunction lifted.

Easy rule: *If you know a parent is violating an injunction related to the school, you should ask the parent to leave, or summon law enforcement.* Although a civil injunction is not criminally enforceable, if it pertains to the school, you should err on the side of protecting the school community.

Modified Orders

Once a final order is put in place setting out the rights and duties of parents and a visitation schedule for the child, that order will be in place until the child turns 18—unless a parent reopens the case by filing a modification. Texas law allows parents to make changes to orders if they can show that there has been a "material and substantial" change in the circumstances of the child or one of the parents *and* that the change they are requesting is in the child's best interest.[8]

Conflicting Court Orders

What if parents give you conflicting written court orders? In one, Mom is entitled to make the educational decision; in the other, Dad is given this right. If this happens, do these two things: (1) make sure the orders have a judge's signature, and (2) look at the date on the order. The most recent one prevails. Recall from above that sometimes parents go back to court to modify a previous order. If this happens, the most recent order governs.

Court Orders Not Yet Reduced to Writing

What if Mom tells you that the judge announced an order today in court, but Mom cannot produce the written order? Mom could be correct. Sometimes months will pass between the time a court orally announces an order and when that order (often 30 or more pages in length) is reduced to writing and signed by a judge.

After a judge has made an oral ruling, the attorney of the prevailing party is typically required to draft the order. The draft order is then sent to the other attorney to be signed. These orders are typically at least 30 pages long, so the drafting, reviewing, approving, and dickering over the details can sometimes take weeks or months. Once the parties agree that the order is drafted according to the court's ruling, the order is sent to the judge for the judge's signature. If the parties cannot agree about what the judge pronounced, then one of the parties must set a hearing in front of the judge so that the judge can sort out the attorneys' differences. All of this red tape takes time.

Technically and typically, these orally announced orders go into effect immediately. Just because the order has not been written and signed doesn't mean it is not yet in effect. News flash: this can complicate things for you and may put you and the school in a difficult position. If a parent tells you that there is a later order that has been announced by a court but has not yet been written, what should you do?

To keep this simple, you could check with Dad to see if he agrees with Mom's interpretation of the oral court order. If Dad agrees, document this and move on. However, if Dad does not agree with Mom's version of the oral court order, you should tell Mom that you will abide by only a written order; then call your supervisor, who should consult with the school attorney. Honestly, you are a campus administrator—you really don't need to be in a position of holding a hearing on the matter in your office with Mom and Dad arguing about what the judge said in court that morning. Besides, you have ARD Committee meetings to attend. You are not required to abide by anything less than a written court order.

Since Mom may be right, however, and since the school should want to abide by the latest and greatest order from the court (written or otherwise), the school attorney should contact the parents' lawyers and ask them to show proof of the judge's recent oral orders. The parents' lawyers may produce a court transcript or other interim proof of the court's oral orders. Often, contact by the school officials or school attorney will encourage the parents' lawyers to get it in gear, draft the order, and get it signed. But at this point you should let the school's central office handle this, and you should rely on advice of the school lawyer. Absent direction from central office and the school attorney, you should request a written order.

Easy rule: *The school's responsibility is to follow the most recent written court orders.* If a parent tells you that there is a recent oral ruling from the court that is not yet written, see if the other parent agrees with the first parent's interpretation of the oral court order, and then document the agreement. If the parents don't agree, the school attorney should contact the parents' lawyers for more information.

Parents Who Agree to Informally Change the SAPCR Order

There are many situations where a divorced parent will agree to allow the other parent certain rights not permitted in the order. As long as these side agreements do not pertain to school safety (such as an order requiring a parent to stay more than 200 yards from school) and as long as the order is not a protective order, such side agreements are actually part of the fabric of family law in the schools. Our conservative advice is to get these side agreements in writing—even in a quick e-mail if you can—to protect against a later claim that you knowingly allowed a court order to be violated. When in doubt or when disputes arise, simply abide by the order.

3. Protective Orders

Protective orders (POs) are issued by courts when there has been violence or the threat of violence in a household or within a family.[9] The purpose of a PO is to protect the physical safety of those named in the order. A PO may protect the children, even if they are not the primary target of the violence. These orders are typically effective for two years but may be permanent.[10] If no expiration date is written on the order, it is valid for two years from the date it is issued.[11] (For an example of a protective order, see appendix C.)

Protective orders will not typically set out decision-making rights of parents as a custody order will, but it will set out a visitation schedule or provide that a parent have no visitation at all with a child.[12] Some usual provisions you will see in a PO are orders prohibiting a parent from:

- Going within a specified distance of the residence, **school,** day care center, or place of employment of a person protected by the order
- Going within a specified distance (typically 200 yards) of a person protected by the order
- Committing family violence
- Communicating in a threatening or harassing manner directly or indirectly with a person protected by the order
- Stalking a person protected by the order[13]

It is not widely known that any adult may file a PO on behalf of any child.[14] Although it would be a rare occurrence, a school employee may request a PO on behalf of a student against a member of the student's family or household, against someone the student is dating, or against someone the student has a child with. In many Texas counties, the county attorney or district attorney assists people in filing for POs free of charge. If you are thinking of filing a PO on behalf of a student, you should first consider whether you must make a report of child abuse or neglect (see chapter 8). You might also consult a private lawyer, the county or district attorney, or the school lawyer.

Once a PO is issued, if a parent or other person is ordered to stay away from the child's school, the clerk of the court should mail a copy of the PO to the school.[15] In reality, this may not happen. If information about where the child is enrolled in school is not provided to the clerk, we should assume the mailing will not occur. If the school is aware there is a PO, but the school has not received a copy from the court, the school should request a copy from the person who obtained the PO, or should request one from the court.

Easy rule: *If a protective order requires a person to stay away from a school, the school should have a copy of the PO.* If the clerk of the court has not sent a copy of the PO to the school, request one from the person who obtained the PO or from the court.

May Parents Agree to Alter or Change a Protective Order?

One thing that distinguishes a protective order from an injunction and other family court orders is that the parties to the PO cannot agree to change or ignore what is in the order.[16] For example, let's say there is a PO in place that provides that Dad has to stay 200 yards away from Sonny's school. Sonny is going to be the star in the school play. Mom and Dad show up at the school together for the play, and Mom tells you that she is fine with Dad being there. Can Dad legally be at the play with Mom's consent? No. For the period that the PO is in effect, only a court can change the PO. The parties cannot agree to change it or even temporarily disregard it. Furthermore, Dad's appearance at the school is a crime,[17] which brings us to another big difference between POs and other sorts of custody orders.

> **Easy rule:** *If you know a parent is violating a protective order related to the school, summon law enforcement.* A PO is criminally enforceable and is not subject to being changed by agreement of the parties.

Protective Orders Are Criminally Enforceable

In the example above, if Dad shows up at the school and law enforcement is called, Dad can be immediately arrested. In fact, if a law enforcement officer observes him in violation of the order, the officer *must* arrest him.[18] Would Mom also be arrested for consenting to the violation of the order? No. Only the person restricted by the PO can be arrested.[19]

Protective Orders versus Civil Injunctions

Finally, it is worth noting that even when there is no PO, there may be a civil injunction enjoining a parent from certain behaviors, including coming to the child's school.[20] We spoke earlier in this chapter about the example divorce decree set forth in appendix B. Take another look at the injunction on pages 35 and 36 of that sample decree. If the father comes to the school outside of his visitation time, he would be in violation of the injunction. The civil injunction is not criminally enforceable—the father cannot be arrested, barring disruptive behavior and so on. However, the school or law enforcement may issue him a criminal trespass warning. After the father has been given a criminal trespass warning, his arrival at the school may lead to his arrest.

4. Guardianship

Another legal mechanism for allowing someone other than the parents of a child to act as the parent is through a guardianship.[21] Although the word "guardianship" is thrown around rather loosely, guardianships are established only by court order. People sometimes use this word when a child has been living with them for some time, even though there are no court orders establishing them as guardians of the child. These relationships are not true guardianships. A true guardianship requires an order signed by a judge. So, if someone arrives at your school claiming to be the guardian of a child, require the person to provide a court order.

Rest assured, guardianships of children are relatively rare. They typically arise when both parents of the child are incapacitated or deceased. A guardian for a child may or may not be a family member.

Guardian of the Person versus Guardian of the Estate

The rights of a guardian are usually listed in the court order, but the order might provide that the guardian has "all the rights granted to a guardian by law." You should review the order to see if the person has been appointed "guardian of the person" of the child. A guardian of the person *generally* has the rights a custodial parent has regarding issues such as educational decisions, residency, medical decisions, and other issues personal to the child. If the guardian has been named only a "guardian of the estate," that guardian's authority extends to financial decisions only, and if he or she is not the parent and does not have guardianship over the person of the child (as opposed to guardianship of the estate of the child), he or she does not have the legal authority to enroll the child in school.[22]

5. Power of Attorney

There are many types of powers of attorney (POAs). A POA allows a person to designate another person to exercise specific rights.[23] For example, you could sign a power of attorney allowing your sister to sell your car. For the purposes of this book, when we refer to a POA, we are referring to a parent who has signed a document allowing a third party to exercise some or all of their rights to their child. Take a look at appendix D, a fairly standard POA related to education. A POA is not a court order, so it will not be signed by a judge. To be valid, it must be signed by the person designating the third party.

There are two important things to note about POAs. First, the document does not limit the rights of the person who signs it. Rather, it expands the number of people who have rights when it comes to the child. Second, a POA may be revoked at any time by the person who granted it.

Let's put those two rules to work in some examples. If Mom signs a power of attorney giving Grandma the power to enroll Mom's child in school, then both Grandma *and* Mom may enroll the child in school. However, if Mom does not have the right in the first place to enroll the child in school (because, for example, that right has been taken away by a court order), then the POA she signed allowing Grandma to enroll the child in school is invalid. Mom cannot grant rights that Mom does not possess.

A POA may be revoked at any time, orally or in writing, by the person who granted it. So in the example above, even if Mom signed a POA allowing Grandma to exercise some of her parental rights, all Mom has to do is say the word, and Grandma will no longer have those rights. If you receive a POA and somehow learn of its oral revocation, it would be best to attempt to obtain an e-mail or other written confirmation of the revocation, even though such action on your part is not required.

6. Authorization Agreement for Nonparent Relative

In 2009 the legislature added Chapter 34 to the Texas Family Code, and then amended it in 2011. This chapter was passed largely in response to the overwhelming number of children living with extended-family members, but without their parents. In many of these situations the families do not have the resources to file lawsuits to deal with legal custody of the children. In the meantime, someone needs to be acting on the child's behalf with schools, doctors, and various other entities. This chapter allows a parent to sign an agreement with *a grandparent, an adult sibling, or an adult aunt or uncle of the child,* authorizing that person to perform certain acts in regard to the child.[24]

The education-related rights the parent can authorize the relative to exercise are these:

- Enrolling the child in a public or private primary or secondary school
- Authorizing the child to participate in age-appropriate extracurricular activities, including athletic activities[25]

Note that this statutorily approved agreement does not go so far as to explicitly set out that the relative who has signed the agreement has the "right to make educational decisions" for the child. Further, if the authorization conflicts with any other law relating to eligibility requirements (e.g., the uncle being authorized to perform certain acts is a registered sex offender who cannot exercise these rights due to other laws prohibiting him from being around children), the agreement is not valid and the other law controls.[26]

The statute is very specific about what the agreement must contain, when a parent may execute one, and the notice required to be given to a second parent who does not sign the agreement.[27] A third party (e.g., school or doctor) relying on an agreement that meets the specifications of the statute is not subject to civil or criminal liability nor is that third party subject to professional disciplinary action.[28] The agreement does not in any way restrict the rights of the parent to continue acting on behalf of the child.[29] It does, however, add to the number of people who can interact with third parties on behalf of the child.

The authorization agreement for nonparent relative is void if executed while there is pending litigation regarding custody, possession, or placement of the child.[30]

The authorization agreement for nonparent relative terminates if, after it is signed, a court enters a SAPCR order; enters an order concerning the custody, possession, or placement of the child; enters an order concerning access to or visitation with the child; or enters an order appointing a guardian for the child.[31] The only way the agreement will remain in effect if a court order is also in effect is if the court grants an order giving written permission allowing the agreement to be in effect.[32]

If the agreement does not indicate when it will terminate, it will remain in effect until revoked.[33] It appears that only a party to the agreement may revoke it. Let's consider some possible situations that could arise.

Scenario: Mom and Dad are separated, but no one has filed a custody suit. Mom signs an authorization agreement for nonparent relative allowing the maternal grandmother to enroll the child in school. Dad does not sign the authorization. Can the maternal grandmother exercise the rights under the agreement without Dad's signature?

Answer: Yes, because Mom has signed the authorization, and no suit has been filed. If a suit is filed, regardless of whether it is filed before or after the agreement is signed, the agreement is not valid unless there is written permission from the court.

Easy rule: *Once a custody suit has been filed, the authorization agreement for nonparent relative becomes invalid, unless written permission from a court confirms the agreement's validity.* It does not matter whether the authorization agreement is signed before or after the custody suit is filed.

Scenario: Same as the above scenario, but now the maternal grandmother is attempting to enroll the child in your school. Dad is attempting to enroll the child in a school down the street. Who gets to enroll the child in school? And can Dad revoke the agreement?

Answer: The question of who gets to enroll the child is a little hard to answer. First, the maternal grandmother, Mom, and Dad would technically have equal rights to enroll the child in school. However, the spirit of this new law allowing parents to delegate is to deal with the situation where there is no parental involvement. Until there is a court order in place, the safest bet would be to let Dad make the call, since he is a parent with an opinion on the subject. As to whether Dad can revoke the agreement, he probably cannot. First, as a general rule, only a party to an agreement can revoke the agreement, and in this example only Mom and the maternal grandmother signed the agreement, Second, Texas Family Code 34.008(e) specifies that if *both* parents have signed the authorization agreement, either parent may revoke the agreement without the other person's consent. The implication here is that only a parent who has signed the agreement may revoke the agreement. Even though it does not appear that Dad can revoke the agreement, we also believe this impliedly means a parent—whether that parent has signed the agreement or not—will ultimately trump the person who is seeking authority under this agreement.

• • •

Scenario: No custody suit has ever been filed. Dad signs an authorization agreement for nonparent relative with his girlfriend, allowing the girlfriend to perform the acts allowed in the statute. Girlfriend arrives with the agreement in her hand to enroll the child in school. Should the school honor the agreement?

Answer: No. The statute is very specific about who may make these agreements. The agreement under this section may be made only between a parent and (1) a grandparent to the child, (2) an adult sibling of the child, or (3) an adult aunt or uncle of the child. So the school would not be able to recognize the document as an authorization agreement for nonparent relative *since the girlfriend doesn't fall into one of those three categories of relatives.*

Like a power of attorney, an authorization agreement for nonparent relative can be revoked at any time. The statute sets out specifically how this revocation should occur.[34] If a parent tells you that he or she has revoked the agreement, but offers no written proof of the revocation of the agreement, ask the parent to provide you something in writing, and dated, indicating that he or she is revoking the agreement. Be sure to keep a copy of this revocation in the child's file, just in case the relative shows up wanting to continue to operate under the agreement.

Chapter 5

Who Has the Right to Pick Up the Child from School, Eat Lunch with the Child, and Attend School Activities and Conferences?

When families are in turmoil, educators can be put in the uncomfortable position of being a referee. And by "uncomfortable," we don't mean like the itchy clothing label scratching the back of your neck. We mean "uncomfortable" like a feeling that makes you want to crawl under your desk and hide. When it comes to the refereeing, remember this: A school administrator is not trained as a judge, a family lawyer, a law enforcement officer, or a marriage counselor. If there is ever a heated or imminent battle between parents (or others asserting the rights of a parent), you should not hesitate to call law enforcement, the school's central office, or the school lawyer, as the case may be, for proper advice and support. As the campus instructional leader, however, you take all the children as you find them, and some of them come from less than perfect environments. You need to be equipped with the basic skill to sort through the less heated conflicts.

The conflict and turmoil sometimes erupt at the most inconvenient times, times meant to be fun events for the student. This chapter gives you some tools to use when some of these common issues arise.

Who Has the Right to Pick Up the Child from School?

The quick and easy answer to this question is that both parents have equal rights to pick up a child from school unless there is a court order limiting that right. Nonparents (including grandparents) do not have the right to pick up a child from school unless a parent has delegated this right to them. If there are court orders in place, the school should request copies of those orders from parents, or the parents' lawyers, and keep them organized so that they are easy to find when needed for reference.

When in doubt about releasing a child:

1. **Check the authorization form.**
2. **Check the court order.**
3. **Check with a known parent.**
4. **Check with the child. (Does the child know this person?)**

Anytime a nonparent picks up a child from school, school personnel must check for the most recent authorization form or the most recent court order. If you are a campus administrator, you must ensure that office staff is clear on this point. This practice will at least minimize misunderstandings and may prevent incidents such as a tragic case in Mississippi.

In *Doe v. Covington County Sch. Dist.*, school personnel released an elementary student, Jane, to Tommy Keyes during the school day on at least six different occasions in the 2007–2008 school year.[1] Each time, he brutally, sexually assaulted her and then returned her to the school, where school employees checked her in.

Keyes' name was not listed on Jane's checkout authorization form, nor was he related to her in any way. There was no court order giving him any rights. He never had any parental, custodial, or guardianship rights whatsoever over her. The court found that "the school repeatedly checked Jane out to this unauthorized stranger, who on multiple occasions signed her out as her father and, on at least one occasion, as her mother!" (exclamation point in court's decision).[2] When a federal appellate court places an exclamation point in its own recitation of the facts, be prepared for a significant legal pronouncement. That is what happened here.

Bear in mind that school employees and school districts are generally immune from liability for student injuries perpetrated by third parties. Barring extreme examples of institutional knowledge of existing harm coupled with deliberate indifference or complicity; or where the student is at the complete and total mercy of the school (the special relationship theory), it is difficult to assign liability to the school or school officials for such injuries. However, on its first review of this case before a three-judge panel, by a 2-1 vote the Fifth Circuit found that the student had a special relationship with the school. Therefore, the court initially determined that the school's gross negligence rose to a level of a constitutional deprivation of the student's right to personal security.[3]

The legal holding in the case was revisited and reversed in 2012 by the entire Fifth Circuit sitting *en banc*, by a vote of 16-2.[4] The court held that the compulsory attendance laws were not enough to create a special relationship between the student and the school to the degree that the school owed the student a constitutional duty to protect her from harm from third parties. This is where this case law stands in the Fifth Circuit. Even though school officials were not held liable, this case is a stark example of the personal harm and the legal troubles that may ensue when school officials release a very young student to an unauthorized person. This is not intended to be a treatise on *Doe* or on school employee liability. However, the case cannot be ignored in a discussion about which adults may pick up students from school.

There are multiple scenarios in which a parent may want to limit who can pick up the child from school. Let's look at a few of the more common ones here.

Scenario: Papa enrolls José in school. Papa does not fill out any information about Mama for the school. José is enrolled in the Extend-A-Care program after school. At the end of the school day, a person we will refer to as "Woman" shows up, claiming to be Mama and wants to leave with José. Papa isn't present. Papa believes José will be going to Extend-A-Care. What should the school do?

Step 1: Woman should be asked for proof that

she is José's mother. Does the school have a copy of José's birth certificate? Can Woman show identification that matches the mother's name on the certificate? If so, "Woman" may in fact be Mama—go to step 2. If not, can Woman show any other legal document allowing her to pick up José, such as a power of attorney? If so, go to step 3.

Step 2: Woman/Mama should be asked if there is any court order regarding parental rights to José. If she produces a court order signed by a judge, it should be reviewed to determine whether Mama has a right to possession of the child under the order (see chapter 4). If the order shows that it is not Mama's time to be with José, go to step 3. If there is *no* court order, Mama should be able to take José, but go to step 3 anyway.

Step 3: Notify Papa that Woman/Mama is there to pick up José. Call Papa no matter which way this plays out. It will save you grief later on. If Papa does not agree to allow Mama to pick up José, and the court order prohibits the school from releasing José to Mama, Woman can be asked to leave. In other words, if the parents are not in agreement, the court order governs this situation. If, on the other hand, Papa says no, but the court order (or other legal document such as a power of attorney) says that Mama can pick up José, then ask Papa if he has a later/greater court order he can produce. If not, tell him that José is going home with Mama and save him the trip to school. If there is no court order, assuming Woman has shown identification that she is Mama, she should be able to take the child.

Step 4: What if Dad cannot be reached? Find out if José recognizes that Woman is actually Mama. Despite all of the proof in the world that Woman is José's mother, it would be troubling to release José to someone who appears to be a stranger to the child. If José doesn't recognize Woman, call the school police or the school's central office, and ask Woman to wait until others can help to sort this out.

Easy rule: *When one parent enrolls a child in school, always ask about the second parent and place a note and any relevant documents, such as court orders, in the child's file.* Doing so will avoid a situation like the one in the scenario regarding José. In that case, Papa should have been asked about Mama and for any court orders regarding the rights and duties to José. If there were no court orders, then the school should let Papa know that if Mama shows up, José will be released to her.

Scenario: Mom is enrolling little Bonnie in school. Mom fills out information about Dad but says that Dad has not been involved in Bonnie's life for years and should not to be allowed to pick her up from school. What should the school tell Mom? If Dad shows up, what should the school do?

Step 1: Mom should be told that unless she has a court order limiting Dad's rights, Bonnie will be released to Dad if he arrives to pick her up. If Mom produces a court order signed by a judge, then whether Dad can pick up Bonnie will be governed by the order. These days most court orders say specifically what days and times each parent has a right to possession of a child (see pages 10–17 of the divorce decree in appendix B, for example). Since Mom has alerted the school to the issues between Mom and Dad, if Dad does show up to pick up Bonnie, the order should be consulted to determine whether Bonnie should be released to Dad. If the order says it is not Dad's time to have Bonnie with him, Dad can be asked to leave.

Step 2: Notify Mom. Knowing of the acrimony between the parents, even if the order says that it is Dad's turn to have Bonnie with him, it is a good idea to call Mom and let her know that Bonnie was released to Dad pursuant to the court order.

Easy rule: *When there is a question about who gets to pick up the child, call each of the known parents for whom you have contact information.* A phone call to each parent now will save you more grief later. Stay focused on asking the parents if they have a valid court order or other legal document that supports their position. Avoid being drawn into the conflict.

What about orders that are not yet written? Sometimes a parent may tell you that a court has issued an order that has yet not been reduced to writing. This is not unusual. Rarely are written orders available on the same day as a court hearing. What is the effect of an order announced by a judge but not yet written? The short and difficult answer for you is that the order may be in effect. (See the section "Court Orders Not Yet Reduced to Writing" in chapter 4 for a discussion of what to do in these circumstances.)

What if each parent produces conflicting, written court orders? First, look toward the last page of the order to see if both court orders are signed by a judge. If so, look to see which was signed last. The date can usually be found near the judge's signature (for an example, see page 38 of the order in appendix B). Rely on the latest court order signed by a judge. If this doesn't solve the issue, punt the parents to central office as described above.

Most orders will say that each parent has the right to the child as they agree and that, failing mutual agreement, the schedule set out in the order will govern. The language may look something like this (see page 10 of the sample divorce decree in appendix B; emphasis added.):

> Mutual Agreement or Specified Terms for Possession
>
> IT IS ORDERED that the conservators shall have possession of the child *at times mutually agreed to in advance by the parties,* and, in the absence of mutual agreement, IT IS ORDERED that the

conservators shall have possession of the child under the specified terms set out in this Standard Possession Order.

These informal agreements between parents happen every day in school settings and do not have to be in writing. If you are not hearing complaints from either parent, then it is working like a charm, as it does 99 percent of the time. The education process, and your career as an administrator, would quickly come to a grinding halt if you and your staff refused to release any student except as strictly set forth in every court order on file. Parents modify these orders by agreement, on the fly, every day, and you and your staff may never even know about it.

However, you may be reading this because there *is* some problem. At the first sign of a problem (e.g., the parent with the right of possession arrives to pick up a child, and the other parent has already done so), let both parents know that if they vary from the possession and access schedule set out in their order, you will need something in writing from the parent whose turn it is to have possession of the child saying that they are allowing the other parent to pick up the child.

As mentioned earlier, parents are not permitted to change the terms of a protective order. If there is a protective order saying, for example, that Mom cannot come with 200 yards of the school, Mom cannot pick up the child from the school. It doesn't matter whether Dad agrees or not. Mom's presence on the school property is a crime, regardless of any agreement between the parties.[5] If Dad tells you that it's fine for Mom to pick up the child from school and there is a protective order prohibiting her from doing so, Dad should be told that you will not be releasing the child to Mom, due to the protective order, and he needs to make other arrangements. (For more information on protective orders, see chapters 2 and 4.)

Easy rule: *Parents can agree to pick up and drop off the child at times not stated in the order.* Parents do this all the time. But note that *parents are not permitted to change the terms of a protective order.*

Scenario: The paternal grandmother (PGM) arrives to pick up little Clem. You call Mom, and Mom objects. Can the PGM take the child?

Answer: The PGM may pick up the child *if* one of the following is true:

1. There is *no* court order in place, and either parent allows the PGM to pick up the child.
2. There *is* a court order in place giving Dad the right to pick up the child at that time, and Dad allows the PGM to pick up the child from school. (Dad may consent by phone call, e-mail, note, or something more formal, such as a power of attorney.)
3. There is a court order in place giving the PGM the right to pick up the child.
4. Neither parent is in the picture, and Clem lives with the PGM. In this case

the PGM is a person standing in parental relation and may pick up the child from school. (In this event, it is not likely that you would know enough of Mom's whereabouts to call her.)

If there is a protective order against the PGM from coming to the school, the PGM may not pick up the child.

• • •

Scenario: Dad's new girlfriend (GF) arrives to pick up the child. What to do?

Answer: The GF's rights to pick up the child are the same as the PGM's in the preceding example.

• • •

Scenario: A biological or adoptive parent (BAP) whose rights have been terminated arrives to pick up the child. What should you do?

Answer: It may be rather obvious, but a BAP whose parental rights have been terminated by a court is a legal stranger to the child; therefore, the BAP would have no right to pick up the child, unless you get consent from the person who *does* have that right to pick up the child—and there is no protective order against the BAP. The terminated parent's rights would be exactly the same as those of the PGM and the GF in the previous two scenarios. Typically, parental rights are terminated due to abuse and neglect. It may seem astonishing that there would be a situation where, *after* a termination, consent would be given for the BAP to pick up the child from school, but this scenario may not be as rare as it sounds. Typically, when Child Protective Services, or CPS (a division of the Department of Family and Protective Services), removes a child from the home because of abuse and neglect, they first try to place the child with relatives. After the dust settles post-termination, sometimes the relative with rights to the child will allow the BAP to be a part of the child's life. So long as the person holding the rights gives consent, and assuming there is no protective order in place against the BAP relating to the school or the child, the BAP may pick up the child from school.

• • •

Scenario: Dad, with a protective order (PO) against him, shows up at school to pick up his child, Thelma. How should the school respond?

Answer: Read the protective order and see if there is any prohibition against Dad being at the school or around little Thelma. There are situations where the court will issue a PO ordering the respondent (in this scenario, Dad) to stay away from Mom and her residence and place of employment but will not order Dad to stay away from Thelma or Thelma's school. So just because there is a PO does not automatically mean that Dad can't pick up Thelma, but proceed with caution—it depends on what the court order says. Some POs will, however, prohibit Dad from going to the school and/or going within a certain distance of Thelma.[6] If the order prohibits either of these things and Dad shows up at the school, law enforcement should be contacted and Dad should not be allowed to pick up Thelma.

• • •

Scenario: Mom (or any other person) shows up drunk to pick up her son Philip. What do you do?

Answer: Allowing anyone who is intoxicated to pick up Philip from school may meet the definition of "abuse" as it is defined by Texas law, and it certainly meets the definition of "neglect."[7] If Mom is apparently intoxicated when she arrives to pick up Philip, contact law enforcement right away and let the police officers sort it out.

• • •

Scenario: Can a school official be liable for keeping a child away from the parent?

Answer: Texas law imposes liability on a person who takes, retains, or conceals the whereabouts of a child at a time when another person is entitled to possession of the child.[8] In addition to imposing liability on the person actually taking, retaining, or concealing the child, Texas law imposes liability on anyone who assists in violating the court order if they had actually seen the court order that is being violated *or* had reason to believe that there was a court order and that it was being violated.[9] This statute is obviously focused on preventing family-related kidnapping, whereby the loser in a court battle employs a network of people to steal the child and disappear. We would find it hard to believe that this statute could be successfully used against a busy school employee who merely misreads a court order. Besides, there are laws protecting school employees from negligence suits when they are acting within the scope of their duties, using their judgment or discretion.[10]

Although there are no reported cases involving school employees, it is conceivable that an angry parent may argue the point. Let's take another look at one of the scenarios above:

Scenario: Mom is enrolling little Bonnie in school. Mom fills out information about Dad but says that Dad has not been involved in Bonnie's life for years and should not to be allowed to pick her up from school. What should the school tell Mom? If Dad shows up, what should the school do?

Answer: If there is a court order in place saying that Dad has the right of possession of Bonnie, Dad has a legal right even if he has not been involved in her life. The school may not intentionally keep the child from Dad in violation of a court order, as personally heartbreaking as that may be in some circumstances. Because the school employee has actual notice of the court order, intentionally keeping Bonnie from Dad under these circumstances could result in an attempt to pursue the employee under these laws. If there is no court order in place, each parent has an equal right to pick up the child.

Who Has the Right to Attend School Activities?

Both parents have the right to attend school activities unless limited by court order. In the vast majority of court orders, both parents will have the right to attend school activities (see page 3 of the divorce decree in appendix B). Usually, the order will say something like this: "it is ordered that, at all times, Mother, as a parent joint managing conservator, shall have the following rights: . . . **the right to attend school activities**. . . ."

The fact that both parents usually have the right to attend can lead to some uncomfortable situations if one or both parents see fit to argue or otherwise cause a scene at a school function. Shame on them. Keep in mind that no parent has a right to be disruptive of the activity. School administrators have a right and a duty to maintain order at a school activity. A parent who is disruptive may be required to leave by a school administrator or by law enforcement. (See chapter 3 for more details about ejecting parents who behave badly.)

Sometimes Parent A will claim that Parent B does not have a right to attend a school activity because it is not Parent B's day to have the child with him or her, according to the court order. This is beside the point. Recall that the right to attend school activities is a specified provision in a court order (page 3 of the order in appendix B). So the real question is whether Parent B has the right to attend school activities. If the answer is yes, then Parent B may attend without regard to whether it is Parent B's period of possession. If the order does *not* specify that Parent B the right to attend school activities, then Parent B does not have that right. Remember, if the court order is silent as to any parent's right, the parent does not own that right. If there is a court order, parents have only the rights listed in the order. In unusual cases, the court order may be very specific about which school activities parents may attend and the parameters under which they may attend those activities.[11] This sort of order is the exception, not the rule, but be aware that such an order might exist.

What Is a School Activity?

Certainly, athletic events, school plays, band competitions, and other activities on school grounds can be considered school activities. But what about the more ambiguous situations, such as an off-campus car wash fundraiser for Band Boosters? There is nothing in the law that defines "school activity" for the purpose of parental rights.

If parents are feuding over the issue of who can come to certain of the child's activities or school events, it may be time to encourage them to go back to court to clarify which parent can come to which activity. One typical outcome of such battles is that the parent who has the right to physical possession of the child at the time of the event will be awarded the right to attend the activity. While this may seem harsh on the parent with the least visitation, it may allow the child the peace of mind knowing that there's no need to worry about a dramatic scene occurring—one that was *not* written into the play in which he or she is performing.

Please, No Beef for Lunch

School lunch can be a contentious time. School lunch sounds a lot like "possession and access" time, and it also sounds like a "school activity," both of which are separately addressed in the court order. What if those two rights collide? What if the parent has one of these rights, but not the other?

Parents have been known to play the lunch card—meaning the parent shows up for lunch when it is technically not their day for possession and access, seeking to gain some advantage over the parent in possession. Or perhaps this parent just digs the school's veal cutlet. In any event, is lunch considered a school activity? Maybe (because it is an activity that children and parents often attend), but the law is not clear.

Scenario: Dad has the right to attend school activities, but does not have the right to possession and access of the child on Tuesdays. Can Dad eat lunch with the child on Tuesday?

Answer: Absent a scene or a disagreement, yes. Lunch may be a school activity and Dad may not be in violation of the order.

• • •

Scenario: Assume the same facts as above, except now Mom and Dad arrive to have lunch with the child on Tuesday, and there is a disagreement. What now?

Answer: You might suggest a solution: have each parent pick a day or two of the week that would be "theirs" for the purpose of school lunch. If the parents are unable to agree on this, they need to go back to court. If their conduct is disruptive, the parents may be required to leave. And if it is truly the veal cutlet that is driving the behavior, offer to ship a box to that parent's house. (We kid.)

• • •

Scenario: Dad is in jail. Mom and Dad never married. The paternal grandfather (PGF) wants to eat lunch with little Elaine. Mom does not like the PGF or Dad. There is no court order. Mom says not to allow the PGF to eat with Elaine. What do you do?

Answer: Despite Dad's incarceration, he still has equal rights to his child, absent a court order. He can also transfer his rights through a power of attorney (see chapter 4) or, in some instances, just by giving permission. If the PGF does not violate school policy or campus security by having lunch with Elaine, and Dad gives his permission, Mom will need to show some other reason to bar this activity.

Who Has the Right to Attend Parent-Teacher Conferences?

If you said something along the lines of "Without a court order in place, both parents have the right to attend parent-teacher conferences," you are on to us—and you are right. If there is a court order, it will usually spell out who has the right to consult with school officials concerning the child's welfare and educational status (see pages 3–4 of the order in appendix B). It will usually say something like this: "it is ordered that, at all times, Father, as a parent joint managing conservator, shall have the following rights: . . . 5. The right to consult with school officials concerning the children's welfare and educational status, including school activities. . . ."

If the order does not specify that a parent has the right to consult with school officials concerning the child's welfare and educational status or the right of access to educational records of the child, the parent does not have that right to attend conferences.

Scenario: The court order says that Parent A can attend school activities, but does not say that Parent A has the right to consult with school officials concerning the child's welfare and educational status. Can Parent A attend the parent-teacher conference?

Answer: If Parent B is not complaining about Parent A's attendance at the parent-teacher conference, then it is safe to assume that Parent A may attend.[12] If Parent B complains about Parent A's attendance at the conference, the big question becomes whether a parent-teacher conference is a "school activity." As set out above, there is no legal definition of "school activity" for the purpose of court orders; however, it is probably safe to assume that a "school activity" is an activity in which the child is participating and to which the parent is invited. If the child is not participating in the conference, the answer is most likely no—Parent A does not have the right to attend the conference. The question is more complicated if the teacher invites children to participate in their conferences. In that case, the safest bet is to allow the parent to attend. However, if the teacher is seeking direction from a parent (i.e., educational decisions), the teacher should look to the parent appointed as the one who has the right to make educational decisions on behalf of the child (see page 6 of the order in appendix B).

Easy rule: *Even if both parents have the right to consult with school officials, offer each parent his or her own conference if having both of them in a parent-teacher conference is too difficult.* Although it will take more time, it will be more pleasant for both the parents and the teacher.

Scenario: The court order gives both parents the right to consult with school officials concerning the child's welfare and educational status. Mom arrives at the parent-teacher conference alone. Dad arrives at the parent-teacher conference with Girlfriend. Can Girlfriend attend the conference over Mom's objections?

Answer: Unfortunately, there is no "right" answer to this question unless the court order specifically addresses this scenario—and every once in a while, you will see one that does. It would be a good idea to have a policy or an administrative rule giving guidance as to what will happen if there is no agreement between the parents. Our best guess is that, absent the consent of both parents, it would be prudent to disallow the attendance of third parties (such as Dad's girlfriend) at parent-teacher conferences, where confidential records will be shown and discussed.

• • •

Scenario: The court order gives both parents the right to consult with school officials concerning the child's welfare and educational status. Mom arrives for the parent-teacher conference. Dad sends Girlfriend to the conference on his behalf. Can Girlfriend attend the conference over Mom's objections?

Answer: There is no legal answer to this question either, unless the court order specifically addresses this situation or unless Dad has signed a power of attorney giving his authority to Girlfriend. If Dad has signed a power of attorney allowing Girlfriend to assume his rights regarding the child, then she may stand in his place and attend the parent-teacher conference. Again, having a policy or administrative rule already in place regarding this sort of situation is desirable. In this case, since Dad is not there in person for the conference, it is probably a good idea that someone be there on his behalf to give him information on the progress of the child. If there is animosity between Mom and Girlfriend, having separate conferences may be the best plan.

• • •

Scenario: Grandparent (GP) shows up alone for the parent-teacher conference. But simply being a grandparent does not give that person rights to a child. Can Grandparent attend the conference?

Step 1: Ask whether there is a court order or power of attorney that addresses whether GP can attend. If there is an order or power of attorney addressing this issue, then it should be followed. If not, go to step 2.

Step 2: Ask whether a parent designated GP as his or her representative for the conference. If there is a parent who has the right to consult with school officials concerning the child's welfare and educational status, and that parent sends GP to the conference, then having the conference with GP in lieu of the parent is fine. If GP has no legal document giving him or her authority to attend the conference, and no parent with the right to consult with school officials concerning the child's welfare and educational status has given permission to allow GP to attend on his or her behalf, go to step 3.

Step 3: Determine whether GP is a person "standing in parental relation." In other words, is GP the person taking care of the child, in the absence of a parent? For instance, does the child live with GP? If so, then GP may be a person standing in parental relation, and the school may conference with GP. If the answer to all three questions is no, then GP should not be privy to the conference without the clear consent of one of the parents.

Chapter 6

Who Has the Right to Make Educational Decisions for the Child?

We reviewed basic parental rights in chapter 3. We all know that one of the basic rights parents have is to make educational decisions for the child. Absent a court order, both parents share equally in making educational decisions for their child. Both parents have equal rights to confer with educators and review their child's records. But what happens when two parents do not agree on educational decisions for the child, and they each look to you for affirmation? This scenario puts educators in the uncomfortable position of trying to placate the grown-ups while doing what is best for the child. In broad terms, there are three scenarios we will discuss in this chapter:

1. Two parents disagree and have no court orders. The parents may or may not be married. They may or may not be getting divorced (although you have your suspicions). But there are certainly no court orders.
2. Two parents disagree and have a divorce decree (they are divorced) or a custody order (they were never married).
3. Third parties acting in the place of a parent.

Parents Disagree and Have No Court Orders

First, we will look at the most difficult of the three scenarios. Two parents disagree, and they have no court orders. This can happen in any number of ways:

- The parents may never have gotten married.
- If they are married, maybe they are separated, with no divorce suit yet filed.
- If they are married, they may not have plans to divorce. They just like to disagree on everything.
- Maybe they are married and have filed a divorce suit, but the suit is so new that there are no court orders.
- Maybe they are not married and have filed a suit affecting the parent-child relationship (a.k.a. custody suit), but the suit is so new that there are no court orders.

In any event, the parents have chosen you over a judge as the first governmental official to hear their vast parental disagreements concerning their child. Amid the uncertainty, two things are for sure: (1) they disagree about their child's education; and (2) there are no court orders. How do you play this hand? Consider this:

Scenario: Junior is struggling in school. Teacher believes that Junior needs special-ed testing. Mom and Dad, whose marriage is still intact, disagree on whether to test Junior. Who gets to make the call here?

Answer: Because the marriage is intact, it is likely that there are no court orders in place describing who gets to have the last say. If there are no court orders, then both parents have an equal say in making decisions for Junior. So what on earth do you do if there are no court orders, but the parents fundamentally disagree with each other regarding the child's education? This certainly places you in a potentially undesirable hot seat. There are no simple answers here; essentially, school officials get to play the reluctant role of tiebreaker. You should do the following:

1. Involve several educators in this process. (Just make sure it is not you alone versus one or both of the parents. Involve the principal, the assistant principal, key teachers, a counselor, and so on, as the case may be.)
2. Take into consideration the conflicting ideas and proposals of both parents.
3. Make consensus-based recommendations or decisions that the educators professionally believe are in the child's best interest.
4. Document the bases for your recommendations or decisions and be prepared to support them with data and explain them.
5. Follow all legal requirements for whatever process is in play—such as Admission, Review, and Dismissal (ARD) Committee meetings, Section 504 meetings, or grievance hearings.
6. Notify your supervisor and/or the school lawyer.

If neither parent agrees with the educators, that circumstance may present a different problem that should be worked out with the school lawyer's advice. Hopefully, one of the parents will agree with the educators' recommendations (or vice versa), and that is the direction in which to proceed. If the other parent disagrees with the school officials, he or she can either hush or seek much needed family court intervention. Court intervention would assist you by giving you future guidance.

• • •

Scenario: Junior is struggling in school. Teacher believes that Junior needs special-ed testing. Dad agrees that Junior should be tested, but Mom disagrees. There are no court orders. Here is the kicker: Mom is in jail. Does Mom still have the right to make educational decisions?

Answer: Yes. Mom may speak from confinement. Being in jail, per se, does not strip away a parent's rights. As a practical matter, it will be more difficult for Mom to voice her opinions, but she still has parental rights equal with those of the father. Expect to see powers of attorney in situations like this. A parent who is locked up in the county jail, for instance, will often execute a power of attorney giving grandparents or some other person his or her parental rights, so that the jailed parent will have a proxy in these matters.

Temporary Orders

When there are no final court orders, temporary orders may be a solution. Even if the parents in the scenarios above had been separated and perhaps even filed suit for divorce, until there are court orders in place spelling out who has the right to make educational decisions, both parents retain that right.

In a custody suit (SAPCR), a parent may request and the court will enter temporary orders, which set out the parents' rights during the custody suit, before a final order is entered. If the parents have a SAPCR on file, you might encourage them (or their lawyers) to seek temporary orders. This will create some peace and order for you in the interim.

> **Easy rule:** *When parents disagree and no court orders exist, encourage the parents to seek temporary orders.*

Family law litigation is expensive. You may find that parents are resistant to ask a court for temporary orders, because they cannot afford it. A contested temporary orders hearing where there is a dispute over children typically adds thousands of dollars in attorneys' fees for each litigant. If no court order is in place, you and your staff will remain in the uneasy position of tiebreaker until a final order is entered.

Parents Disagree and Have a Divorce Decree or Custody Order

Now we will look at the scenario in which the parents are divorced or were never married, but they have a court order in place regarding the child. We would think this would lead to situations that would be easier to decipher, and usually they are. However, in some situations described below, court orders may be of little help.

Scenario: Junior is struggling in school. The teacher believes that Junior needs special-ed testing. Mom and Dad are divorced, and there is a court order saying Mom and Dad may consult with school officials, but Mom has the exclusive right to make educational decisions. Does Dad get to have any say at all?

Answer: Yes, Dad gets to have a say. But Mom gets to make the decision. Most court orders require that the parents consult with one another before making a decision concerning the health, **education,** and welfare of the child (see, for example, pages 3–6 of the order in appendix B). However, in this scenario, Mom has the ultimate right to make the decision, which is what the school can focus on. The school does not have to investigate whether Mom has consulted with Dad prior to making the decision. Bottom line: Mom gets to make the call. Note also that there are many rights and duties listed in divorce decrees involving education (see chapter 1). However, the most important right when it comes to resolving issues about the child's education is *the right to make educational decisions.*

• • •

Scenario: Junior is struggling in school. The teacher believes that Junior needs special-ed testing. Mom agrees that Junior should be tested. Dad disagrees. Mom and Dad are divorced, and there is a court order saying that both Mom and Dad have the right to make educational decisions, subject to the agreement of the other parent. Who gets to make the call here?

Answer: For the purposes of making educational decisions, when you have parents who cannot come to an agreement (and there are *lots* of parents who fall into this category), this order is as good as no order at all. Therefore, the same answer set out in the first scenario above would apply: you get to be the reluctant tiebreaker again.[1]

• • •

Scenario: The scenario is the same as the preceding one, except that there is a court order saying that both Mom and Dad have the right to make educational decisions, *independently* (i.e., Mom can make the decision, and Dad can make the decision, and neither has to agree with the other). Who gets to make the call here?

Answer: You are unlikely to see many orders of this type. They are robustly frowned upon in family law circles. However, sometimes parties will agree to this provision in a shortsighted attempt to save money and/or avoid a contested hearing. People who agree to such a provision in an order do not anticipate the problems that can arise later. An order providing for each parent to make independent educational decisions could lead to a situation, for example, where each parent enrolls the child in a different school, which is of course unworkable. Again, this order is as good as no order at all when the parents do not agree. If this is the order you are dealing with, you once again end up as the reluctant tiebreaker.

• • •

Scenario: Junior is struggling in school. The teacher believes that Junior needs special-ed testing. Mom agrees that Junior should be tested. Dad disagrees. Mom and Dad are divorced, and there is a court order saying that both Mom and Dad have the right to make educational decisions, subject to the agreement of the other parent. Subsequent to the divorce decree being entered, a two-year protective order was issued against Dad, requiring him to stay 200 yards away from Junior at all times, as well as 200 yards away from Junior's school. Does Dad still have the right to make educational decisions?

Answer: The short answer to this question is yes.[2] Although Dad may not come up to the school, he still retains all rights that are not specifically taken away by the protective order. As a practical matter, it may be harder for Dad to exercise this right (because he will not be able to attend ARD Committee meetings or parent-teacher conferences on campus), but he will be able to continue making decisions from afar, pursuant to the divorce order.[3] We learned earlier that many jailed parents will execute a power of attorney, essentially deputizing another person to stand in their place, while they serve time. Can Dad in this example execute a POA? No, he cannot. A person can transfer only rights that he or she has. If Dad in this example does not have the right to be present within 200 yards of Junior's school, Dad cannot execute a POA giving another person this right. So Dad will not have a proxy at ARD Committee meetings and so on, unless school officials and the Mom consent.

Third Parties Acting as Parents

Finally, we will explore situations in which a third person (a.k.a. a person standing in parental relation[4]) is interacting with the school on behalf of the child. Typically, a school should be dealing with parents when it comes to matters regarding children attending the school. Sometimes parents are absent from the child's life for a variety of reasons (death, jail, substance abuse, mental illness, job demands, etc.). In these situations a grandparent, aunt, uncle, or friend may step into the place of the parent in taking care of the child. This situation is common enough that the Texas Education Code recognizes it.[5]

Scenario: Grandparent has enrolled Junior in school. Grandparent is the only person the school has interacted with regarding Junior. Junior is struggling in school. The teacher believes that Junior needs special-ed testing. Can the school ask Grandparent to make the decision about whether Junior should be tested?

Answer: From the brief facts given above, it appears that Grandparent is a "person standing in parental relation" and would be able to make the decision about whether to have Junior tested.[6] Schools officials have to be able to communicate with an adult about the children they are educating. Ideally, this would be a parent, but in some situations a parent is not in the picture. The answer to this example would be a little less clear if the school had brief encounters with either parent. If either or both parents had interacted with the school, the school should first attempt to contact the parents. If there is no parent in the picture, they can rely on Grandparent's decision.

• • •

Scenario: Junior is struggling in school. The teacher believes that Junior needs special-ed testing. Mom and Dad are divorced, and there is a court order saying that Mom has the right to make educational decisions. Dad is dead set against special-ed testing. Mom has signed a POA giving the maternal grandmother (MGM) authority to exercise all of Mom's rights. The MGM shows up at a meeting to discuss the issue of special-ed testing. Does the MGM have the authority to consent to the testing over the protests of Dad?

Answer: Yes. Mom has the sole right to make educational decisions. Mom authorized the MGM to exercise her rights via a POA. The MGM can now act on behalf of Mom. The MGM can consent to the testing on Mom's behalf over Dad's protests. If Mom frequently delegates her rights to another person, perhaps Dad can go to court and seek modification of the order. For now, the MGM trumps Dad.

• • •

Scenario: Junior is struggling in school. The teacher believes that Junior needs special-ed testing. Mom and Dad are divorced, and there is a court order saying that Mom has the right to make educational decisions. Mom objects to special-ed testing. Mom has signed a POA giving the maternal grandmother (MGM) authority to exercise all of Mom's rights. The MGM shows up at a meeting to discuss this issue. Does the MGM have the authority to consent to the testing over the protests of Mom?

Short answer: No. Mom gets to make the call. If Mom has made the school aware of her opposition to Junior's testing, Junior should not be tested. POAs give additional people the authority to exercise the rights of the person granting the power. POAs do not limit the rights of the person granting their authority to a third person (see the section "Power of Attorney" in chapter 4). In other words, if Mom grants a POA to the MGM, that means that both Mom *and* the MGM have the right to make educational decisions. However, a POA may be revoked at any time by the person signing it. Therefore, Mom is the person with the right to make educational decisions, so her right to object to the testing is superior to that of the MGM. Incidentally, if Mom opposes the decisions the MGM is making on behalf of the child, Mom should revoke the POA by notifying the school (and anyone else who has relied on the document) and by destroying the original document.

• • •

Scenario: Junior is struggling in school. The teacher believes that Junior needs special-ed testing. Mom and Dad are divorced, and there is a court order saying that Mom has the right to make educational decisions. Mom is dead set against special-ed testing. Mom signed a POA giving the maternal grandmother (MGM) authority to exercise all of Mom's rights but later called the school to say that she no longer wanted the MGM to make decisions on behalf of Junior. The MGM shows up at a meeting to discuss the issue of special-ed testing, and Mom does not. Does the MGM have the authority to consent to the testing over the protests of Mom?

Answer: No. A person who grants a POA to a third person may revoke it at any time. Sometimes it is revoked by destroying the document. Other times it is revoked by informing the school in writing or orally. Once the school has been given notice that Mom has revoked the POA, school personnel should no longer allow the MGM to make decisions on behalf of the child. It would be a good idea for Mom to memorialize the revocation in writing, even if it is just a signed and dated handwritten note for you to put in the file.

Chapter 7

Who Has the Right to the Child's School Records?

We know from chapter 3 that parents can review and access student records. When it comes to determining who is a parent, we will leave that discussion firmly planted in chapter 2. If you wonder whether Grandma, Pee-Paw, or some other person might be able to view a student's records, please revisit chapter 2. Here, we take a quick look at the laws affecting the release of student records and emphasize some of the aspects of family law that become intertwined with student records.

> **Easy rule:** *All parents are entitled to review and access their child's education records, unless restricted by a court order or law.* This is one of the most basic rights of every parent.

The Legal Framework

The *Family Educational Rights and Privacy Act* (FERPA) is a federal law and the primary source of authority for student record confidentiality. The focus of FERPA is in its name: privacy. Student records are confidential, or private, and may be released only to an authorized person, unless permission is granted by a parent. FERPA is found at Title 20 United States Code Section 1232 (et seq.).

The *Texas Public Information Act* (TPIA) is the state law that controls the disclosure of public records. It may be accessed in the Texas Government Code, Chapter 552. The TPIA sets forth the premise that all governmental records are public, unless specifically excepted from that status. Of course, student records are excepted, meaning they are confidential and can be disclosed only to a parent or other authorized person. Here is the relevant provision:

> Sec. 552.114. EXCEPTION: STUDENT RECORDS.
> (a) Information is excepted from the requirements of Section 552.021 ["Availability of Public Information"] if it is information in a student record at an educational institution funded wholly or partly by state revenue.
> (b) A record under Subsection (a) shall be made available on the request of:
> (1) educational institution personnel;
> (2) the student involved or the student's parent, legal guardian, or spouse; or
> (3) a person conducting a child abuse investigation required by Subchapter D, Chapter 261, Family Code.

The *Texas Education Code* provides that a parent is entitled to access all written school district records concerning the parent's child, including the following:

- Attendance records
- Test scores
- Grades
- Disciplinary records
- Counseling records
- Psychological records
- Applications for admission
- Health and immunization information

- Teacher and counselor evaluations
- Reports of behavioral patterns[1]

The *Texas Family Code* contains a stock provision that is included in most divorce decrees and custody orders. Recall the three tiers of conservatorship (decision-making) rights found in a divorce decree: (1) decision-making rights at all times; (2) decision-making rights during periods of possession of the child; and (3) decision making of the "Big Rights." These were discussed in more detail in chapter 1. The right to access a child's educational records is almost always going to be a right that a conservator may exercise "at all times," unless modified by the court.[2]

It is obvious that state and federal laws all point to the generalized view that parents are entitled to access and to review their child's educational records.

FERPA

The Basics

FERPA is a lengthy, tedious law. This chapter is not meant to be a treatise on FERPA, but we will strive to hit some of the high points. The U.S. Department of Education (DOE) is the enforcing agency over FERPA and has implemented numerous regulations interpreting and enforcing it. In December 2008 the DOE adopted amendments to FERPA regulations. FERPA regulations may be accessed at Title 34 Code of Federal Regulations, Part 99.[3]

A "school official," as that term is used in FERPA and defined by the school district, may review student records without the parent's permission, if the school official has a "legitimate educational interest" in reviewing the records. The 2008 regulations broaden the term "school officials" to include "a contractor, consultant, volunteer, or other party to whom an . . . institution has outsourced . . . services or functions."[4] The outsourced service provider must be under the control of the school in order to be a "school official." This new regulation seems to clarify that FERPA confidentiality is not triggered by volunteers who assist teachers in grading, even if the volunteers have access to the grade book, as long as the volunteers are under the direct control of the teacher and the school.

As stated above, in order to review the records, a school official must have a "legitimate educational interest." The new regulations tighten up what had apparently been loosely defined over the years. No longer does every school employee have a right to review every record of every student at the school or in the district. Districts must now use reasonable barriers (physical, technological, or administrative, as through an enforced administrative policy) to restrict access to information to only those school officials who have a legitimate educational interest in the information.[5]

Computerized grading systems must be secured so that teachers will have access only to their students' records. The comments to the new regulations state that "if a parent or eligible student alleges that a school official obtained access to the student's records without a legitimate educational interest, the burden is on the district or institution" to show otherwise.[6] There must now be a tangible nexus between the employee and the need to access a particular student's records.

> **Easy rule:** *Education records may be reviewed by school officials (as designated by school policy) who have a legitimate educational interest in reviewing them.* Parental permission need not be sought.

It is widely known that the school may charge a statutory fee for searching records and for making copies under the Texas Public Information Act. This is where the TPIA and FERPA differ. FERPA is much more expansive in allowing parents to access and even copy records, often without the school charging a fee. FERPA provides that a school may *not* charge a fee for searching for student records. The school *may* charge a nominal fee for copies, but *may not charge a fee* if the fee "effectively prevents a parent or eligible student from exercising the right to inspect and review the student's education records."[7]

Parental Rights under FERPA

FERPA specifically states that each parent has the right to inspect and review student records, unless the school has been given evidence that there is "a court order, State statute, or legally binding document relating to such matters as divorce, separation, or custody that specifically revokes these rights."[8] This is where our family law topic comes into play. While FERPA is the granddaddy of student records laws, it defers to restrictions put in place by court orders and state family laws.

A parent can also ask to amend a school record that the parent believes contains information that is inaccurate, misleading, or in violation of the student's rights of privacy.[9] Further, the school must give parents annual notification of their rights under FERPA, including the following:

- The right to review and inspect their child's records (and the procedure for doing so)
- The right to seek amendment of the records (and the procedure for doing so)
- The right to consent to disclosure of the records
- The right to file a complaint with the Department of Education for the school's failure to comply with FERPA
- The right to know who a "school official" is and what a "legitimate educational interest" is, so that parents will know who has access to their child's records[10]

So let's consider the court orders that we've been discussing in this book. Will student records be addressed in a divorce decree or custody order? Yes, they will. The right to access educational records is one of the specific rights that will always be seen in such a court order. It is specifically addressed in the Texas Family Code as one of the rights the conservators will have at all times, absent a limitation by the court. It will usually be stated something like this in the decree: "it is ordered that, at all times, Mother [or 'Father'], as a parent joint managing conservator, shall have the following rights: . . . **the right of access to medical, dental, psychological, and educational records of the children**" (see pages 3–4 of the divorce decree in appendix B).

If this right is *not* listed in a court order, the parent's rights to access student records under FERPA, the TPIA, and the Texas Education Code cease to exist.

> **Easy rule:** *A divorce decree or custody order will trump a parent's rights to access student records under FERPA, the TPIA, and the Texas Education Code.*

Unless restricted by law or a court order, a parent or eligible student must be given the opportunity to inspect and review the student's education records within a reasonable period of time, but not more than 45 days after it has received the request.[11]

Scenario: Mother and Father divorce. The divorce decree lists the right of access to medical, dental, psychological, and educational records of the children in Father's list of rights but is silent as to whether Mother has this right. Mother comes to school asking to see the child's TAKS scores. Can you show Mother the scores?

Answer: In this example, Mother does not have the right to the educational records of the child. This question is covered in chapter 1 by the following easy rule.

Easy rule: *A parent has only the rights attributed to that parent in the court order.* Said another way, if a right is not listed in the court order, the parent does not have that right. Said yet another way, a court order is not likely to affirmatively state that a parent does *not* have a right; rather, it will simply be omitted from that parent's list of rights. It doesn't matter what the right is or what kind of conservator the parent is. If the right isn't listed, the parent doesn't have it.

The FERPA rights of parents transfer to the student once the student has reached 18 years of age or attends a postsecondary institution and thereby becomes an "eligible student."[12]

Health and Safety Emergencies

The pre-2008 FERPA regulations allowed for disclosure of confidential information in an emergency and further stated that emergencies must be strictly construed. The 2008 regulations now state that if the school determines there is "an articulable and significant threat to the health or safety of a student or other individuals," it may disclose information from education records to appropriate parties whose knowledge of the information is necessary to protect the health and safety of the student or other individuals. The DOE will not question the judgment of the school as long as the school's decision is rational.[13]

Parents Are Entitled to Their Child's Records—Not the Records of Other Children

If a parent's request for his or her child's records would also drag into the net the records regarding another child, then the other child's information must be de-identified.

Scenario: The school custodian of records is subpoenaed to court. The subpoena requires the custodian to bring "any and all records of student Jane Doe." All of the pages of attendance records for Jane Doe also reflect the attendance of every other child in the class. Should the custodian of records bring the attendance records to court?

Answer: Yes, but all of the identifying information for the other students should be redacted or de-identified (e.g., using a heavy duty black magic marker, correction fluid, or something more high-tech) to remove all identifying information about students other than Jane Doe.

What Are Student Records?

Education records, as defined in FERPA, include records that are

1. Directly related to a student

and

2. Maintained by an educational agency or institution or by a party acting for the agency or institution[14]

Note that this is a fairly broad category of documents. It is not just academic records and disciplinary records but potentially any kind of record maintained by the school.

Among the types of documents *not* included as education records in FERPA are the following:

- Records that are kept in the sole possession of the maker, are used only as a personal memory aid, and are not accessible or revealed to any other person except a temporary substitute for the maker of the record
- Records of the law enforcement unit of the school district
- Records created or received by the school after an individual is no longer a student in attendance and that are not directly related to the individual's attendance as a student.
- Grades on peer-graded papers before they are collected and recorded by a teacher.[15]

As you may have already anticipated, there can be student records under FERPA that are not student records under the Texas Education Code, and vice versa. For instance, FERPA may *exclude* counselor notes from the definition of records, if they are notes "kept in the sole possession of the maker, are used only as a personal memory aid, and are not accessible or revealed to any other person except a temporary substitute for the maker of the record."[16] But Texas Education Code Section 26.004 *specifically includes* counselor records as being available to parents.

Is this a conflict? No. A conflict only arises when one law says a parent *shall* get the records, and another law says the parent *shall not* get the records. Here the Texas Education Code just seems to go further in its definition of student records. Normally, in such a case the parent gets the benefit of the expansive definition, but this may not be true for counselor records, which have been the subject of legal discussions in recent years.

May a Parent Access a Counselor's Records?

Counselor records have the potential to be a hot potato in a family law case. Consider the school counselor who spends lots of time with a child whose family is involved in a contentious divorce and custody battle. Consider further that if abuse or neglect or potential student suicide is involved, there could be a parent or a lawyer who may be very interested in the counselor's records.

What if releasing the counselor's records may endanger the child? Carrying our discussion forward from the last section, it seems that a parent will have access to counselor records unless there is a conflict—in other words, unless another law or court order says the parent shall *not* receive them. Is there such a law? Potentially, yes. The Texas Health and Safety Code states:

> The professional [counselor] may deny access to any portion of a record if the professional determines that release of that portion would be harmful to the patient's physical, mental, or emotional health.[17]

Section 611.001(2) of that code defines a "professional" as one of the following:

- A person authorized to practice medicine in any state or nation
- A person licensed or certified by this state to diagnose, evaluate, or treat any mental or emotional condition or disorder
- *A person the patient reasonably believes is authorized, licensed, or certified as provided by this subsection*

So, do parents get the school counselor's records or not? It depends. Such was the issue posed to the Texas attorney general who sorted through the conflict and concluded that parents do indeed get the counselor records, unless **each** of the following conditions applies:

1. The counselor is a licensed professional counselor (LPC) who received his or her license under the Texas Occupations Code;
2. The counseling records were made for the counselor's private use as a memory aid and were not accessible to any other person except a temporary substitute; and
3. The counselor has determined that release of the records would be harmful to the patient's "physical, mental, or emotional health."[18]

The attorney general compared the duties and obligations of an LPC with those of a counselor certified by the Texas Education Agency (TEA) and concluded that only the LPC's records are confidential in these circumstances. If your school counselor is not an LPC and is certified only by the TEA, the Texas Health and Safety Code does not protect against disclosure of such records.

But note that a "professional" under Texas Health and Safety Code Section 611.001(2) is also "a person the patient reasonably believes is authorized, licensed, or certified as provided by this subsection." Does a student know or even care whether the school counselor is certified under the Texas Occupations Code or by the TEA? Might the student "reasonably believe" that there is no difference between a school counselor and an LPC? These issues might have to be considered in a sensitive case.

Another factor that could further complicate a particular situation is that a counselor does not necessarily need a parent's permission to counsel a child in some circumstances. The Texas Family Code provides that a licensed or certified counselor who reasonably believes that a child has been sexually, physically, or emotionally abused, is contemplating suicide, or is suffering from a chemical or drug addiction or dependency may counsel the child without the consent of the child's parents.[19] Whether this provision applies to

Easy rule: *A parent is* not *entitled to counselor records if three conditions apply:*

1. The counselor is a licensed professional counselor (LPC) who received his or her license under the Texas Occupations Code.
2. The counseling records were made as a memory aid for the counselor's private use and were not accessible to any other person except a temporary substitute for the counselor.
3. The counselor has determined that release of the records would be harmful to the patient's "physical, mental, or emotional health."

a school counselor who is certified by TEA (and is *not* an LPC) is an open question. If it does, an odd scenario could arise whereby the counseling sessions may be confidential, but the counseling notes are not. Suffice it to say that if you or your school counselor ever believes that releasing records might endanger a child's safety, it would be wise to consult the school lawyer, who may be able to present the matter to a court.

School Records and Missing Children

Many missing children are the victims of family abduction.[20] State law requires a person enrolling a student younger than age 11 in the public schools to provide information about the child's previous schools. If the person does not provide this information, the school shall report this fact to law enforcement before the 31st day after the person fails to provide the information.[21]

If the school is notified that one of its former students is a missing person, the school has a duty to inform law enforcement if and when a person requests records pertaining to that student. Further, the school may not advise the requesting party that the request pertains to a missing person.[22] (These important obligations are set out fully in note 22.)

Scenario: Dad enrolls eight-year-old Sonny in school. The alert school clerk informs Dad that he must provide information about Sonny's previous schools. Dad fails to provide the requested information. What should the school do?

Answer: Because Dad did not provide the requested information about Sonny's former schools in a timely manner, the school will have no option but to report this fact to law enforcement on the 30th day after Sonny was enrolled.

Chapter 8

When and How Do I Report Child Abuse and Neglect?

Suspected child abuse or neglect is a topic that may very often be intertwined within a family law case. Whether the alleged abuse or neglect occurs at home, school, or elsewhere, if it involves schoolchildren, it could involve you. It seems all educators know that suspected child abuse or neglect must be reported within 48 hours to an appropriate law enforcement agency.[1] So important is this legal duty that failure to report child abuse or neglect is a crime.[2] It is one of the rare instances in law when your mere possession of certain knowledge of criminal activity is in itself a crime, if not reported.

> **Easy rule:** *If a certified or licensed school employee has reason to believe that abuse or neglect of a child has occurred or may occur, the employee must make a report.* If it is an emergency, call 911 or your school district police. If it is not an emergency, call the Texas Abuse Hotline at 800-252-5400, or go to www.txabusehotline.org and fill out an electronic reporting form.

Consider this: While it certainly seems to be our moral duty to report our knowledge of certain events, *not* calling the police to offer your description of a car accident you witnessed is not a crime, as long as you were not a participant in the accident. Likewise, it is not a crime to refuse to report descriptions of suspects fleeing a bank robbery that you just witnessed—again, assuming you had nothing to do with the robbery. We live in a free society and there is no penalty for *not* turning in your neighbor with the suspicious-looking plants and the grow lights in his basement. The government cannot force you to turn in your neighbor or anyone else—unless suspected child abuse or neglect is involved.[3] Even though you had absolutely nothing to do with the actual abuse or neglect, your mere knowledge of it now makes you culpable. This has been attacked in court as an alleged violation of the First Amendment, to no avail. (Q: Can the government make me say something I may not want to say? A: Yes.)[4]

Let's begin with a discussion that defines "abuse and neglect" and describes an educator's responsibility to report.

What Are Child Abuse and Neglect?

It is advisable for every educator to regularly review the legal definitions of child abuse and neglect, and certainly at the beginning of each school year. It should be a regular part of your school's in-service training. This will give educators a better grasp of what the state considers to be child abuse or neglect. Here are the definitions found in the Texas Family Code: "Abuse" includes the following acts or omissions by a person:[5]

1. Mental or emotional injury to a child that results in an observable and material impairment in the child's growth, development, or psychological functioning
2. Causing or permitting the child to be in a situation in which the child sustains a mental or emotional injury that results in an observable and material impairment in the child's growth, development, or psychological functioning
3. Physical injury that results in substantial harm to the child, or the genuine threat of substantial harm from physical injury to the child, including an injury that is at variance with the history or explanation given and excluding an accident or reasonable discipline by a parent, guardian, or managing or possessory conservator that does not expose the child to a substantial risk of harm
4. Failure to make a reasonable effort to prevent an action by another person that results in physical injury that results in substantial harm to the child
5. Sexual conduct harmful to a child's mental, emotional, or physical welfare, including conduct that constitutes the offense of continuous sexual abuse of young child or children under Texas Penal Code Section 21.02,[6] indecency with a child under Texas Penal Code Section 21.11,[7] sexual assault under Texas Penal Code Section 22.011,[8] or aggravated sexual assault under Texas Penal Code Section 22.021
6. Failure to make a reasonable effort to prevent sexual conduct harmful to a child
7. Compelling or encouraging the child to engage in sexual conduct as defined by Texas Penal Code Section 43.01[9]
8. Causing, permitting, encouraging, engaging in, or allowing the photographing, filming, or depicting of the child if the person knew or should have known that the resulting photograph, film, or depiction of the child is obscene as defined by Texas Penal Code Section 43.21 or pornographic
9. The current use by a person of a controlled substance as defined by Texas Health and Safety Code Chapter 481 in a manner or to the extent that the use results in physical, mental, or emotional injury to a child
10. Causing, expressly permitting, or encouraging a child to use a controlled substance as defined by Texas Health and Safety Code Chapter 481
11. Causing, permitting, encouraging, engaging in, or allowing a sexual performance by a child as defined by Texas Penal Code Section 43.25

"Neglect" includes the following acts or omissions by a person:[10]

1. Leaving a child in a situation where the child would be exposed to a substantial risk of physical or mental harm, without arranging for necessary care for the child, and demonstrating an intent not to return by a parent, guardian, or managing or possessory conservator of the child
2. Placing a child in or failing to remove a child from a situation that a reasonable person would realize requires judgment or actions beyond the child's level of maturity, physical condition, or mental abilities and that results in bodily injury or a substantial risk of immediate harm to the child
3. Failing to seek, obtain, or follow through with medical care for a child, with the failure resulting in or presenting a

substantial risk of death, disfigurement, or bodily injury or with the failure resulting in an observable and material impairment to the growth, development, or functioning of the child

4. Failing to provide a child with food, clothing, or shelter necessary to sustain the life or health of the child, excluding failure caused primarily by financial inability unless relief services had been offered and refused
5. Placing a child in or failing to remove the child from a situation in which the child would be exposed to a substantial risk of sexual conduct harmful to the child
6. Placing a child in or failing to remove the child from a situation in which the child would be exposed to acts or omissions that constitute "abuse" under subdivisions 5–8 or 11 above committed against another child
7. The failure by the person responsible for a child's care, custody, or welfare to permit the child to return to the child's home without arranging for the necessary care for the child after the child has been absent from the home for any reason, including having been in residential placement or having run away

Modification of the Definitions of Abuse and Neglect in the School Setting

Special modifications apply to the definitions of abuse and neglect if the abuse or neglect is alleged to have occurred in a school setting.[11] Abuse and neglect in this context do *not* include the following:

1. Use of restraints or seclusion that do not meet the statutory definitions of child abuse or neglect
2. Actions that school personnel or volunteers at the child's school reasonably believe to be immediately necessary to avoid imminent harm to self or other individuals, if the actions are limited only to those actions reasonably believed to be necessary under the existing circumstances (The actions do not include acts of unnecessary force or the inappropriate use of restraints or seclusion, such as use of restraints or seclusion as a substitute for lack of staff.)
3. Reasonable physical discipline (Reasonable physical discipline is appropriate to the child's age and development and the reason for which the discipline is being administered and is without physical injuries that result in substantial harm or without genuine threat of substantial harm from physical injury to the child.)[12]

What Is Indecency with a Child?

As can be seen, the definitions of abuse include references to several other criminal statutes that define certain crimes against children. One of the references is to "indecency with a child," as defined by Texas Penal Code Section 21.11. That section is specifically referenced in two additional places in the body of the law requiring educators to report abuse. The law directing that a report shall be made says:

> If a professional has cause to believe that a child has been abused or neglected or may be abused or neglected, or that a child is *a victim of an offense under Section 21.11, Penal Code,* and the professional has cause to believe that the child has been abused as defined by Section 261.001 or 261.401,

> the professional shall make a report not later than the 48th hour after the hour the professional first suspects that the child has been or may be abused or neglected or is *a victim of an offense under Section 21.11, Penal Code.*[13]

"Indecency with a child" is a crime that is but one part of the definition of "abuse" that must be reported. What is indecency with a child? Here is a shortened version of that statute of the Texas Penal Code:

> Sec. 21.11. INDECENCY WITH A CHILD.
>
> (a) A person commits an offense if, with a child younger than 17 years and not the person's spouse, whether the child is of the same or opposite sex, the person:
>   (1) engages in sexual contact with the child or causes the child to engage in sexual contact; or
>   (2) with intent to arouse or gratify the sexual desire of any person:
>   (A) exposes the person's anus or any part of the person's genitals, knowing the child is present; or
>   (B) causes the child to expose the child's anus or any part of the child's genitals.
>
> (b) It is an affirmative defense to prosecution under this section that the actor:
>   (1) was not more than three years older than the victim and of the opposite sex;
>   (2) did not use duress, force, or a threat against the victim at the time of the offense; and
>   (3) at the time of the offense:
>   (A) was not required under Chapter 62, Code of Criminal Procedure, to register for life as a sex offender; or
>   (B) was not a person who under Chapter 62 had a reportable conviction or adjudication for an offense under this section.

As you can see, "indecency with a child" covers a wide range of sexual conduct involving children under the age of 17, including perhaps the most pervasive form of sex in the schools: consensual sex between minors.

Do I Need to Report Consensual Sex between Minors?

A question that arises in many in-service trainings on the subject of child abuse and neglect is this: "Do I have to make a report if I have reason to believe that a 16-year-old student is having consensual sex with another 16-year-old student, outside of school?" This is a good and difficult question. The very short—and very conservative—answer is yes. Here is why: If we look at the statute above, we can see that technically, such an act constitutes "indecency with a child," requiring a report, because the statute addresses any kind of sex involving children under the age of 17. A closer look reveals that it is a defense to that crime if the persons are no more than three years apart in age and of the opposite sex; if there was no force, threat, or duress; if neither person is a registered sex offender; and if neither person has been convicted of certain sex crimes. How can you be sure of all of this? The mere fact that you have come to believe, for whatever reason and with enough reliable information, that a student younger than 17 is having sex is probably reason enough to make the report. It *may* protect the child, but it *will* protect you from being accused of failing to report.

It appears that the basic, underlying purpose of the "indecency with a child" statute is to criminalize sexual conduct between a child less than 17 years old and a person more than three years older than the child. As a baseline, this is what we want to make sure gets reported. If every educator makes a report of every instance they know or suspect is understood to be consensual sex between teens less than 17 years old and within three years of each other's age, many, many reports might be made. As a practical matter, this may or may not serve a meaningful purpose. In fact, the Department of Family and Protective Services is not required to investigate a report that alleges child abuse or neglect by a person *other than a person responsible for a child's care, custody, or welfare.* Instead, the appropriate state or local law enforcement agency investigates that report if the agency determines an investigation should be conducted.[14]

Child Protective Services has specific rules that govern when a CPS investigation will take place regarding abuse or neglect occurring in a school setting. All of the following criteria must be met:[15]

1. The allegations must meet the definitions of abuse or neglect.
2. The alleged perpetrator must be a person meeting the definition of school personnel or volunteers at the child's school.
3. The alleged victim must be a child or must have been a child at the time that the alleged abuse or neglect occurred.
4. The alleged abuse or neglect must have happened in a school setting.
5. The alleged abuse or neglect must have occurred during the current school year or there must be a likelihood that sufficient evidence can still be obtained to establish whether or not abuse or neglect occurred in a school setting.
6. The same allegations involving the school setting must not have already been investigated by CPS.

If a report of alleged abuse and neglect does not meet these criteria, it is referred to an appropriate law enforcement entity or other investigating agency. When a report is not accepted for investigation, CPS must notify the reporter verbally or in writing as to the reason the report will not be investigated and must inform the reporter that he or she may discuss concerns about the decision with the CPS supervisor.

Easy rule: *Your duty to report is broader than the duty of CPS to investigate.* Even if CPS may not investigate, you are still required to report.

As you can see, CPS is more concerned with abuse and neglect of children at the hands of their caretakers, whether the caretaker is a parent, stepparent, grandparent, guardian, teacher, principal, other school employee, or other institutional employee. CPS might choose not to investigate a report of a 16-year-old having consensual sex with another 16-year-old off campus. Reporting it will, however, keep you from being accused of failing to report. Depending on the circumstances and the facts at hand, you might consider other administrative remedies or solutions in such a case (such as contacting the parents or counseling the students) in addition to making a report.

All of the above assumes we are talking about your knowledge of sexual activity between minors occurring *outside of school*. When you have knowledge of any student's sexual activity taking place *during school, at school events, or on the bus,* this requires reporting and a prompt administrative response, which should include appropriate discipline, among other important considerations.[16] Even if CPS does not investigate, law enforcement will.

Furthermore, the above discussion assumes we are talking about teens engaging in sexual conduct. The tone of our answer changes when the children are younger. Any kind of sexual conduct by preteen or prepubescent children simply strikes a different chord regardless of the age of the other person involved, and the need to report becomes an unequivocal and not-so-conservative yes, in addition to other administrative strategies that you will employ.

What about Sex between a Minor and an 18- or 19-Year-Old?

So that we can be clear, the statute regarding "indecency with a minor" is initially triggered anytime a person younger than 17 engages in sexual conduct with another person. It criminalizes this behavior if one of the persons is more than three years older than the other. So if the difference in the ages of the persons is less than three years, it is possible that no violation has occurred even though one person is 14 and the other one is 17, depending on their birth dates. Or 15 and 18. Or 16 and 19. You get the picture. Should you report anyway? As above, our very conservative and very short answer is yes.

Does This Mean I Don't Have to Report Sexual Conduct of a 17-Year-Old?

It appears that 17-year-olds are excluded as potential victims from the "indecency with a child" provision. However, 17-year-olds are still "children"—minors—for all other purposes of the definitions of abuse and neglect. Whether you will report sexual activity on the part of a 17-year-old will depend on your fact base and whether the abuse or neglect provisions are triggered.

Who Is Required to Report?

Easy rule: *Every certified or licensed school employee who has direct contact with children, and has reason to believe that child abuse or neglect has occurred or may occur, must report within 48 hours.*

Without regard to our education, profession, or other status, we *all* have a duty to report suspected child abuse and neglect. In fact, the law states that we *all* have the duty to "immediately" report child abuse and neglect.[17] This includes lawyers, even if the lawyer learns from a client that the client has abused or neglected a child. This is yet another stark example of just how important it is to report. All otherwise rock-solid common-law privileges evaporate when a lawyer, doctor, or clergy member learns of child abuse from a client, patient, or penitent.[18] The privilege does not protect the otherwise confidential conversations of the lawyer, doctor, or clergy. Like everyone else, members of these professions must report.

Furthermore, in a proceeding regarding the abuse or neglect of a child, evidence may not be excluded on the ground of privileged communication, except in the case of communications between an attorney and a client.[19] We take this to mean that while lawyers, doctors, and priests have to report abuse committed by their clients, patients, and penitents, doctors and priests may be made to further testify against their patient or penitent. Lawyers may not be compelled to testify against their clients.

More to the point for your purposes, the law singles out some "professionals" who specifically work with children and assigns to these professionals a heightened duty to report within 48 hours.[20] These professionals include the following:

- Teachers, nurses, doctors, day-care employees, employees of a clinic or health care facility that provides reproductive services, juvenile probation officers, and juvenile detention or correctional officers
- Any other individual "who is licensed or certified by the state or who is an employee of a facility licensed, certified, or operated by the state and who, in the normal course of official duties or duties for which a license or certification is required, has direct contact with children."

We construe this to include all school employees who are in some way licensed or certified by the state and who have direct contact with children. This obviously includes principals, teachers, counselors, diagnosticians, other campus administrators, nurses (RNs and LVNs), and certified teacher aides.

Are Bus Drivers Required to Report within 48 Hours?

Perhaps less obvious, the definition of professionals who specifically work with children also includes school bus drivers—workers not always considered to be "professionals" in school parlance. Bus drivers are, after all, licensed by the state, and they have direct contact with children in the normal course of their official duties. It's pretty clear that they are included in the heightened requirement to report within 48 hours. Yet, at a transportation department in-service training we conducted several years ago, the transportation director standing in the back of the room interrupted the training and "corrected" our interpretation of this reporting provision. He told his bus drivers *not* to make reports but rather to come to him and *he* would make the report. Astonished, we politely but firmly "uncorrected" him in front of all the drivers, to which he replied that this would be further discussed after our departure. On the car ride home, we diagnosed the transportation director as having unresolved control issues and predicted that the incident would cause us never to be invited back. Ever. We were correct.

Bus drivers may be in a unique position to witness conduct on a bus or at a bus stop that does not occur on campus. Therefore it is imperative that bus drivers understand their role and their duty to report. At least one case has included bus drivers among the potential witnesses to child abuse.[21] If a bus driver suspects sexual conduct occurred on the bus, the driver should report this to the supervisor *and* make a report to the authorities.

May the Report Be Delegated to Someone Else?

The attitude of the transportation director mentioned above is somewhat understandable: folks who have risen to the ranks of administrator (whether as a principal or a transportation director) might be fairly characterized as people who like being in charge. This is not necessarily a bad thing. If no one wanted to be in charge, we would all wander around aimlessly, muttering to ourselves, and nothing would ever get done. Someone has to be in charge, to give direction and guidance to the potential that exists within the human spirit—and it might as well be you. Yet some people in charge want all information to flow through them and to be approved by them. This is where child abuse and neglect reporting requires administrators to "let go." Other persons who report to school administrators and are also licensed by the state (such as teachers, counselors, certified aides, bus drivers, etc.) have an independent, nondelegable duty to report.

Time and again during in-service trainings on this topic, when we ask, "To whom must you make a report?" an educator in the room will respond, "To my principal" or "To the counselor." This is wrong. This is a myth that must be dispelled. As an administrator, you must make it clear at all staff trainings that the duty to report is nondelegable, and it is your responsibility as an administrator to respect the legal obligations of your staff. However, we suggest in trainings that it makes sense to let the boss or counselor know that such a report is being made. Principals have been known to go into a bit of a snit when their first knowledge of a report occurs when the deputy sheriff shows up in the office wanting to question students. It is advised that teachers and other school employees apprise their supervisors when a report is made; or better yet, make the report together.

May a Teacher Who Makes a Report over an Administrator's Objection Be Reprimanded?

A professional who makes a report in good faith, or who cooperates with an abuse or neglect investigation, may not be retaliated against by an administrator and may not receive any kind of employment sanction. Recall that "professional" means any licensed or certified school employee, including bus drivers. An employee who is retaliated against for reporting child abuse or neglect may sue the school district, and normal governmental immunities are waived for this purpose. In many respects, the employee/plaintiff is treated very much like a whistle-blower.[22]

Thus, if a transportation director fires a bus driver for making a report without first obtaining the director's permission, the bus driver may sue the district and recover damages, court costs, attorneys' fees, and reinstatement—an expensive proposition for the school district. Proving that the legislature has thought of everything, these legal remedies do not apply to an employee who reports abuse or neglect committed by the reporting employee.[23]

What Is the Penalty for Failing to Report?

Failing to report child abuse or neglect is a class A misdemeanor.[24] This carries a maximum penalty of up to one year in jail, a $4,000 fine, or both.[25] There are no reported criminal decisions against school employees for failure to report. Keep in mind, however, that court decisions are usually not reported until they are appealed. Trials in the Texas state courts, including pretrial dispositions, are not reported in a way that can be efficiently researched. So the absence of a reported case does not mean that school employees have not been investigated by CPS or law enforcement for alleged failure to report. On the contrary, our experience allows us to say with certainty that this happens fairly regularly, and probably more so today than even 10 years ago. In fact, anecdotally it seems that when the abuse or neglect occurs on school grounds, at school events, or at the hands of school employees, administrator conduct will be scrutinized by CPS in light of the allegations.

Consider this example. The school administrator receives an allegation from a school employee or a parent, accusing another school employee of abusing a student. Instead of reporting the alleged abuse within 48 hours, the administrator initiates his or her own investigation, taking several days to complete it. Regardless of whether the principal finds for or against the accused, CPS and law enforcement may subsequently second-guess the principal's assessment of the original allegation and conclude that a report should have been made sooner.

Further, even if neither CPS nor law enforcement takes action, the school district might move to terminate employment, or the Texas Education Agency (TEA) might seek to sanction an educator's certificate. In one case, the principal of a middle school was terminated by the school district for alleged failure to report child abuse perpetrated by a teacher on his campus, after the principal was given evidence of the illicit and illegal relationship between the teacher and a student. Because the principal failed to report, he was arrested, prosecuted, and terminated from employment.[26]

Can I Be Sued for Failing to Report?

Let's suppose you have reason to believe that a teacher has abused a student on your campus and you fail to timely report it. We know that can be considered a crime. Can you also be sued by the parents? Yes, the parents can sue you, but the better question is whether you will win or lose. In 1998 the Texas Supreme Court held that failing to report child abuse pursuant to the statutory reporting requirement is not negligence, in and of itself.[27] The court concluded that there is no civil cause of action for failing to adhere to the requirements of the statute, a decision that left open the possibility of a cause of action for a common law duty to report. A later court concluded, however, that if such a common law duty existed, educators would be immune from liability due to the general immunity laws that apply to school employees.[28]

While there is no recognized private cause of action for failing to report, there are other ways in which failure to report could continue to be legally complicated. In another case, a teacher was sued because she knew of abuse being perpetrated on a student by a coach, and she failed to report. While the civil rights claims against her were dismissed (because she was neither the perpetrator nor the coach's supervisor), her failure to report kept her involved in the litigation.[29]

Supervisors are liable only for the conduct of their subordinates, however, if the supervisor knows that a student's constitutional rights are being violated and the supervisor acts with "deliberate indifference." We must assume that a student's constitutional rights are violated anytime a school employee abuses a minor/student. In yet another case, a principal was told from a variety of sources that a coach was having an affair with a minor/student. The principal was even shown love notes written by the coach to the student. The principal allegedly did very little, if anything, to respond to this information. The court concluded that the principal could be considered to have been "deliberately indifferent," making the principal potentially liable for the student's injuries.[30]

What If I Don't Know Whether to Report? What Is the Standard for Reporting?

Easy rule: *When in doubt, report.* This is admittedly very conservative advice, but if you are asking the question, then you should err on the side of reporting.

A report should reflect the reporter's belief that a child has been or may be abused or neglected or has died of abuse or neglect.[31] This is not a subjective standard. Rather, it is a "reasonable person" standard. This means that the reporting requirement is triggered by a "reasonable" cause to believe that a child's physical or mental health or welfare has been, or had potential to be, adversely affected by abuse or neglect. Instead of reviewing your subjective knowledge, a court will try to ascertain what a "reasonable" person of ordinary intelligence and experience would think.[32] Not to suggest that any of us are anything less than reasonable and ordinary.

A person making a report must identify, if known, (1) the name and address of the child; (2) the name and address of the person responsible for the care, custody, or welfare of the child; and (3) any other pertinent information concerning the alleged or suspected abuse or neglect.

To Whom Do I Make a Report?

The statute says that a report shall be made to (1) any local or state law enforcement agency; (2) the Department of Family and Protective Services or Child Protective Services; (3) the state agency that operates, licenses, certifies, or registers the facility in which the alleged abuse or neglect occurred; or (4) the agency designated by the court to be responsible for the protection of children.[33]

Easy rule: *In an emergency, call 911 or your school district police. In non-emergencies, call the Texas Abuse Hotline at 800-252-5400, or go to www.txabusehotline.org and fill out an electronic reporting form.* This website is also a great place to go for more information about child abuse and neglect.

Your statutory duty to report is also satisfied anytime you report to a badge-wearing, gun-toting law enforcement official.

Is My Report Confidential? Can an Angry Parent Find Out I Made a Report?

Unless you waive confidentiality, your report is supposed to be confidential.[34] It may be disclosed to a law enforcement officer for the purposes of conducting a criminal investigation of the report. However, we have worked on cases where the identities of the educators were not kept confidential by CPS, or the identities were so obvious that redacting (or de-identifying) was ineffective. This is a problem, it is a reality, and there are no good solutions.

Information concerning the reported abuse or neglect must be provided by the Department of Family and Protective Services to the parent, managing conservator, or other legal representative of a child who is the subject of reported abuse or neglect. Under the relevant section of the Texas Family Code, a report shall be released to a parent if the department has edited it to protect the confidentiality of the identity of the person who made the report and any other person whose life or safety may be endangered by the disclosure.[35]

Can I Be Sued by an Angry Parent for Making a Report?

It is conceivable that an angry parent could sue you for making a report, assisting in an investigation, or testifying against the parent. As long as your conduct is in good faith, you are immune from liability.[36] More importantly, if a court dismisses a case filed against you after deeming it frivolous, unreasonable, or without foundation because you are immune from liability, you may be awarded attorney's fees and litigation expenses against the plaintiff.[37]

As you might expect, child abuse reporting can sometimes be used as a tool for harassment in a divorce or custody suit, and you might somehow be dragged into it. If a party to such a suit makes a report alleging child abuse by another party to the suit that the reporting party knows lacks a factual foundation, the court shall deem the report to be a knowingly false report. This outcome is admissible in a suit between the involved parties regarding the terms of conservatorship of a child, and the offending party may be fined.[38]

What Can I Expect with an Abuse or Neglect Investigation in a School Setting?

Prior to conducting an investigation in a school setting, CPS must notify the school principal (or the principal's supervisor if the principal is an alleged perpetrator) that a report has been assigned for investigation and must specify the nature of the allegations contained in the report, as well as the date and time when the investigator plans to visit the school campus to begin the investigation. The CPS investigator must request that the school principal (or the principal's supervisor) *not* alert the alleged perpetrator or others regarding the report until the investigator has first had an opportunity to interview the alleged perpetrator.[39] Keep in mind that this applies only to a CPS investigation, and not to a law enforcement investigation.

A CPS investigation conducted in a school setting will include a series of investigative steps, unless the allegations of child abuse and neglect can otherwise be clearly confirmed or ruled out.[40] CPS will seek to accomplish the following:

1. Obtain a full statement of the allegation from the reporter, as appropriate to the case.
2. Interview or examine each alleged victim, as appropriate in the case.
3. Interview any other witnesses or persons who may have collateral information, including the child's parents or guardian.
4. Interview the alleged perpetrator, when available.
5. Obtain photographs, school records, or other pertinent physical evidence, if relevant to the investigation.
6. Request that a parent of an alleged victim obtain a medical, psychological,

or psychiatric examination of the child and that the records of such examination be provided to the CPS investigator, if necessary, to properly investigate the allegations in the case.

7. Request that the alleged perpetrator submit to a medical, psychological, or psychiatric examination and that the records of such examination be provided to the CPS investigator, if necessary, to properly investigate the allegations in the case.
8. Cooperate with law enforcement in the event that law enforcement is conducting a joint investigation regarding the allegations.
9. Conduct a criminal history background check on the alleged perpetrator.
10. Complete the investigation, reach a disposition as to each allegation made in the report, and submit the investigation report and findings to a CPS supervisor for approval within 30 days after initiating the investigation, unless an extension of time is approved by the worker's CPS supervisor due to extenuating circumstances.
11. Close the investigation, if it becomes apparent after initiating it that the allegations made in the report do not, in fact, meet one or more of the criteria for investigation specified in 40 Texas Administrative Code Section 700.404 (see the section "Do I Need to Report Consensual Sex between Minors?" above).
12. Send a copy of the completed report of the department's investigation to the Texas Education Agency, the State Board for Educator Certification, the local school board or the school's governing body, the superintendent of the school district, and the school principal or director, unless the principal or director is alleged to have committed the abuse or neglect, for appropriate action.[41]

School officials or other persons related to the school setting may not interfere with a CPS investigation. Interviews and examinations in a school investigation may take place on or off the school premises, as deemed appropriate by CPS, provided the investigator notifies the school principal (or the principal's supervisor if the principal is the alleged perpetrator) before conducting an interview or examination on school premises.[42]

CPS may request that school personnel or volunteers not be present during the interview or examination of an alleged victim, an alleged perpetrator, an adult or child witness, or any other person who may have information relevant to the investigation if the investigator determines that one of the following circumstances pertains:

- The presence of school personnel or volunteers would compromise the integrity of the investigation.
- A better interview or examination of the child would result without school personnel or volunteers being present.[43]

Finally, at the first contact with the parents or with the alleged perpetrators, the CPS investigator must do the following:

1. Identify himself and have the Texas Department of Protective and Regulatory Services (TDPRS) identification available for inspection.
2. Explain the nature of the complaint or the reason for the contact.
3. Explain TDPRS's role and legal

responsibilities in the investigation.
4. Discuss each allegation in the report.
5. Ask for a response to the allegations or an explanation of the alleged victim's situation in light of the report.[44]

While the law states that a school employee may not interfere with an investigation, the campus principal can and should remain engaged to the extent possible with any investigation happening on campus. If law enforcement arrives on campus and calls teachers into a meeting with rival parents of the two children who allegedly engaged in sexual misconduct, should the teachers be made to "tell all" in front of *both* sets of parents, possibly violating confidentiality standards? A principal might suggest to law enforcement that the teachers be interviewed separately, out of the presence of the rival parents. If a principal at any time believes that CPS or law enforcement is acting in a heavy-handed way, the principal should immediately summon assistance from the central office and the school lawyer.

If I Am Accused, Do I Have to Talk to CPS or Law Enforcement?

There may be employment penalties for not talking to CPS or law enforcement, but anyone accused of a crime cannot be compelled to talk. If you feel that you are, or could reasonably become, the focus of the CPS or law enforcement investigation, you should not talk to anyone without first seeking the advice of a lawyer. Even though a CPS investigator does not wear a badge or tote a gun and does not have the right to arrest, that does not lessen the gravity of a CPS investigation.

What If I Have Been Wrongfully Determined to Have Caused Abuse or Neglect of a Child?

Like school employees, Child Protective Services workers do God's work and are underpaid. They are responsible for protecting the lives and safety of children and for making rapid determinations about whether a child is in danger or has been abused. However, their resources and time are never adequate, and sometimes errant conclusions are made. It is not uncommon for CPS to wrongfully conclude that a teacher or administrator contributed to the abuse or neglect of a school student. The possible scenarios are endless:

- A principal receives a complaint of alleged abuse by a teacher and conducts her own investigation before reporting. Her investigation takes several days. By the time she reports, it has been more than 48 hours, and CPS concludes that the principal is guilty of "neglect" and "failure to report."
- A principal receives information about two elementary students engaging in sexual antics on the playground, and calls the parents and CPS. Even though the principal was not on the playground, she is accused of "neglect" by CPS, for inadequate supervision.
- An assistant principal administers corporal punishment according to policy but is accused of abuse the next day by the parent. CPS concludes that the assistant principal is responsible for abuse.

> **Easy rule:** *Do not administer corporal punishment to schoolchildren even if your school district allows it.* Administering corporal punishment exposes you to potential civil and criminal liability.

At the end of a CPS investigation, CPS will make one of three findings: (1) there was "reason to believe" a certain person was responsible for abuse or neglect; (2) a person is not responsible for abusing or neglecting a child (i.e., is "ruled out"); or (3) CPS is "unable to determine" whether a person abused or neglected a child. Please note that CPS cannot do anything to you as an educator. CPS cannot take your students away from you, cannot sue you, cannot take your certificate, and cannot prosecute you for a crime. However, if CPS errantly concludes there is "reason to believe" that you are responsible for abuse or neglect, this could negatively affect all of the above: (1) the school district might attempt to fire you; (2) the TEA might take action against your certificate; (3) the county or district attorney might charge you with a crime; and (4) the CPS conclusion might give fuel to a civil action against you.

You will want to quickly obtain a copy of the CPS report. The law states that CPS shall provide a copy of the report of the investigation to the parent, managing conservator, or legal guardian of a child who is the subject of the investigation *and to the person alleged to have committed the abuse or neglect.*[45] The report of the investigation should be edited to protect the identity of the persons who made the report of abuse or neglect.

If CPS errantly concludes there is "reason to believe" you are somehow responsible for abuse or neglect of a child, this conclusion can be appealed through a procedure called an administrative review of investigative findings (ARIF). To be timely, the request must be filed within 45 days of the CPS decision, so time is of the essence.[46] Unless a civil or criminal court proceeding or a criminal investigation relating to the alleged abuse or neglect is pending, the Department of Family and Protective Services will conduct the ARIF by the 45th day after receiving the request. If a civil or criminal court proceeding or an ongoing criminal investigation is pending, the department may postpone the review until the court proceeding is completed. If you do not challenge the findings, the findings will become final and will stay on your record indefinitely.

Chapter 9

Help! I've Been Subpoenaed! What Do I Do?

It is at least unnerving, maybe even frightening, when you are minding your own business, doing your job, and an official-looking person shows up and hands you official-looking papers requiring you to go to court in a custody case.[1] Although this will be inconvenient and maybe scary, it is an important part of the legal process. Not only is it important to the process, but complying with a subpoena is required by law.[2]

Additionally, all school district employees are entitled to paid leave, without penalty, while complying with a valid subpoena.[3] A subpoena may kick you out of your comfort zone, but at least you will not miss any pay, and you will be able to return to your job in due time.

In custody litigation, the adults get to put on evidence for the court. Children often do not have anyone to speak for them or to even give the court unbiased information on how they are faring as their parents are splitting up. Since school employees spend more of a child's waking hours with them during the week than the parents, school employees are often key witnesses in custody litigation. That's where you come in.

What Does the Court Want to Know?

If it makes you feel any better, here's a secret—judges *love* school employees. Since you are probably not the dad's buddy or the mom's relative, and your job is to educate children, you will be seen as someone who knows a *lot* about children generally and a *lot* about this child in particular *and* as someone who does not have an interest in the outcome of the litigation. In other words, you probably do not have an ax to grind. You will be a rare, unbiased witness in the case. As such, your information may be given significant weight by the court in making its decision. Usually, the information sought from a school employee will be the answers to questions such as these:

- How is the child doing academically and socially in school?
- Have you seen any changes in the child's behavior? If so, can you recall when those changes began?
- How many times has the child been tardy or absent, if any?
- Who brought the child to school on the days the child was tardy? (Or what days of the week is the child typically late/absent from school?)
- How many times has the child been absent from school?
- Were the absences excused or unexcused?
- Has either parent been late picking the child up from school? If so, how often? When? Why?
- Is the child clean and appropriately dressed for the weather when he or she comes to school?
- Does the child typically have assignments

completed on time? If not, are there particular days of the week when this is a problem?

- Who typically signs homework, report cards, and so on?
- Who attends parent-teacher conferences and/or ARD Committee meetings?
- How does the child react when each parent drops off or picks up the child from school? Does the child appear to have a preference for either parent?
- Does either parent volunteer at the school? If so, how often, and for what?
- Has either parent or the child behaved in a way that causes you concern?

One of the reasons testifying may be uncomfortable is that the information you give to the court may be unfavorable to one or both parents—parents with whom you are required to have a professional relationship as their child's teacher, counselor, coach, principal, or other role. While you are testifying, your duty is to tell the truth. Witnesses are immune from collateral lawsuits for truthful testimony in court. Any statements made in the trial of any case, by anyone, cannot constitute the basis for a defamation action.[4] Keep in mind that you did not make the facts. You are just giving very important information the court needs to make a decision that is in the best interest of the child.

In some cases, the attorney may ask you with whom you think the child should live? This question typically gets at the heart of the litigation. If you have an opinion on the matter and no objection is made or sustained, you may answer it honestly.[5] If you do not have an opinion, you may tell the court that as well.

How Much Notice Will I Be Given?

There is no hard-and-fast rule regarding how much notice is required before a witness can be subpoenaed to court.[6] The summoning party must have been "diligent" in its efforts to obtain your testimony.[7] What is considered to be diligent will depend on the circumstances. If you have any concerns about the amount of notice given or any other issue surrounding your testifying in the case, contact your school's lawyer.

Do I Have to Comply with a Faxed Subpoena?

Technically, you don't have to comply with a subpoena that is delivered by fax. But you may agree to receive a subpoena by fax to expedite the process. In order to be compelled to show up when subpoenaed, all of the following must be true.

1. The witness must be served with the subpoena by someone who is over the age of 18 but is not a party to the lawsuit.[8]
2. A $10 witness fee must be delivered with the subpoena.[9]
3. The location to which the witness is subpoenaed must be within 150 miles of the county where the witness lives or is served.[10]

The people who serve subpoenas charge the requesting party money for each subpoena served—anywhere from $50 to $100, depending on the circumstances.[11] As a practical matter, when witnesses are "friendly," a lawyer may ask them if they will accept a faxed subpoena in order to keep litigation costs down.[12] Most friendly witnesses need only a subpoena to show their employer. If you do agree to accept a subpoena via fax, e-mail, or some other method, you should comply with the subpoena. You do not, however, have to agree to accept this informal method of service.

What Can Happen If I Don't Show Up to Testify?

If you do not show up at the place and time set out in a properly served subpoena, the court can hold you in contempt—which means imposing a fine and/or ordering you to jail.[13] Further, the court may issue an order requiring law enforcement to pick you up and bring you to the courthouse.[14] Therefore, subpoenas should *not* be ignored. If you have a good reason not to comply, you should contact the school lawyer or your personal lawyer as soon as possible after you are served.

Do I Have to Bring Documents with Me to Court?

The subpoena should clearly state whether you are required to bring documents with you when you appear in court. If it does require you to bring documents, it should state clearly which documents you need to bring. Typical wording on a subpoena will say that you are required to bring "any and all documents regarding Jane Doe." That means you are required to bring any documents in your possession or subject to your control regarding Jane Doe. If you feel that any of the documents are sensitive and need to be kept confidential or you have other questions about what documents to bring, talk to the school's lawyer about your concerns.[15]

Sometimes the "custodian of records" of the school will be subpoenaed. This person is in charge of keeping all the written records of the children attending the school. In this circumstance the subpoena will request that all of the child's school records be produced. The purpose of having the custodian of records appear in court will typically be to prove to the court that the documents produced are authentic—in other words, that these are *really* the child's school records. Typically, the custodian of records will not be asked other information about the child's behavior unless the custodian has firsthand knowledge of the parties or the child.

What Can I Expect When I Go to Court?

Most lawyers will not subpoena witnesses to court without first talking with them to find out what they will say. You will probably have a good idea about the questions you will be asked by the party subpoenaing you before you get to court, unless the party or the party's attorney has been unsuccessful in attempting to contact you. When the party who subpoenaed you asks you questions, that process is called direct examination.

When direct examination is over, the other party (the party that did not subpoena you) will have a chance to ask you questions. This part of the process is called cross-examination. Most good lawyers understand this rule: It is rarely a good idea to attempt to skewer an objective school employee in cross-examination.

Easy rule for the family lawyer: *Think very carefully before trying to stick it to a school employee!*

Here are some tips for going to court:

- Dress professionally.
- Make sure you know how to get to the courthouse, where to park, and where you are going once you get inside the courthouse.
- Be punctual.
- Do not talk to other witnesses or the parties about the case while waiting to testify. You may talk to the attorneys.[16]
- Bring something to do (reading, knitting, cell phone) because you may be spending some time sitting out in the hallway, waiting your turn to testify.
- Once you go into the courtroom, put away anything you brought to do (especially the cell phone), and focus on what is happening in the courtroom.
- When you are called to testify, the only documents you should take up to the stand with you are the documents the subpoena requires you to bring, if any. Nothing more.
- While testifying, listen to the question asked, and answer only that question.[17]
- If you do not understand the question you are being asked, ask that the question be repeated or rephrased.
- If you do not know the answer, "I don't know" is a perfectly fine answer—unless you are being asked your name of course (that answer would be viewed as sassy). If you are asked your opinion and do not have one, "I do not have an opinion about that" is an acceptable answer. If you are asked a question and do not remember, "I don't remember" will suffice. There is only a requirement to tell the truth. There is no requirement to know the answer to every question.
- If a question is asked and there is an objection, wait quietly until the judge sustains or overrules the objection—and try to enjoy the drama and suspense. Do not try to rush in your answer over the objection. If the objection is sustained, do not answer the question. If the objection is overruled, you may answer the question. If your answer draws an objection, do not take it personally. It is just part of the process. If you are unsure about what to do after an objection and a ruling from the court, just ask the judge.
- Tell the truth.

Although no one enjoys being questioned in court, and it might even be a little unpleasant or boring, your participation is in fact a linchpin in our democracy. We have all made a social contract to use the court system to resolve disputes that cannot otherwise be settled. Nonparties such as fact witnesses and members of the jury have to step up from time to time to keep the wheels of justice spinning in the right direction.

School employees play a unique role here, because everyone knows you have already devoted your life to the service of others. Testifying in court is just an infrequent extension of that service. You have information about how the child is adjusting, not only because you know about the child's academic performance, but also because you spend lots of time with the child. You are not expected to take the stand and testify "for" one of the parents. You are expected to testify *about the child*, so that the court may do what is in the child's best interest. Keeping that in mind may make what at first seems like an unpleasant, intimidating or boring experience, a rather important and honorable one.

Appendix A: Order of Termination of Parental Rights

NO. D-1-FM-08-123456

IN THE INTEREST OF	§	**IN THE DISTRICT COURT**
	§	
CHILD	§	**98TH JUDICIAL DISTRICT**
	§	
A CHILD	§	**TRAVIS COUNTY, TEXAS**

ORDER OF TERMINATION

1. *Date of Hearing*

On January 10, 2009 the Court heard this case.

2. *Appearances*

Petitioner, State of Texas, appeared in person and through attorney of record, Attorney, and announced ready for trial.

Respondent, Mother, appeared in person and through attorney of record, Another Attorney, and announced ready for trial.

Respondent, Father, appeared in person and through attorney of record, Yet Another Attorney, and announced ready for trial.

Also appearing was Child's Attorney, appointed by the Court as attorney ad litem of the child the subject of this suit. The attorney ad litem has agreed to the terms of this order, as evidenced by the signature of the attorney ad litem below.

3. *Jurisdiction*

The Court, after examining the record and hearing the evidence and argument of counsel, finds that it has jurisdiction of this case and of all the parties and that no other court has continuing, exclusive jurisdiction of this case. A request for identification of a court of continuing, exclusive jurisdiction has been made as required by Section 155.101. All parties

1

entitled to citation were properly cited.

4. Jury

A jury was waived, and all questions of fact and of law were submitted to the Court.

5. Record

The record of testimony was duly reported by the court reporter for the 98th Judicial District Court.

6. Child

The Court finds that the following child is the subject of this suit:

Name: Child
Sex: Male
Birth date: October 20, 1999

7. Termination

Mother.

The Court finds by clear and convincing evidence that Mother has knowingly placed or knowingly allowed the child to remain in conditions or surroundings that endanger the physical or emotional well-being of the child.

The Court also finds by clear and convincing evidence that termination of the parent-child relationship between Mother and the child the subject of this suit is in the best interest of the child.

IT IS THEREFORE ORDERED that the parent-child relationship between Mother and the child the subject of this suit is terminated.

Presumed Father.

The Court finds by clear and convincing evidence that Father has engaged in conduct or

2

knowingly placed the child with persons who engaged in conduct that endangers the physical or emotional well-being of the child.

The Court also finds by clear and convincing evidence that termination of the parent-child relationship between Father and the child the subject of this suit is in the best interest of the child.

IT IS THEREFORE ORDERED that the parent-child relationship between Father and the child the subject of this suit is terminated.

8. Social Study

The Court finds that the required preadoptive social study has been made and is on file. The Court further finds that the social study meets the requirements of the Court.

9. Interstate Compact

The Court finds by clear and convincing evidence that Petitioner has filed a verified allegation or statement regarding compliance with the Interstate Compact on the Placement of Children as required by section 162.002 of the Texas Family Code.

10. Managing Conservator

IT IS ORDERED that State of Texas is appointed Managing Conservator of the child the subject of this suit, the Court finding this appointment to be in the best interest of the child.

IT IS ORDERED that State of Texas shall, each twelve months after the date of this order, file with the Court a report of facts concerning the child's welfare, including the child's whereabouts and physical condition.

11. Costs

IT IS ORDERED that costs of court are to be borne by the party who incurred them.

3

12. *Medical History Report*

The court finds that Mother has prepared a medical history report that addresses the medical history of Mother and Mother's ancestors.

13. *Medical History Report*

The court finds that Father has prepared a medical history report that addresses the medical history of Father and Father's ancestors.

14. Record Sealed

IT IS ORDERED that all papers and records in this case, including the minutes of the Court, be sealed.

15. Relief Not Granted

IT IS ORDERED that all relief requested in this case and not expressly granted is denied.

This Order of Termination judicially PRONOUNCED AND RENDERED in court at Austin, Travis County, Texas, on January 10, 2009, and further noted on the court's docket sheet on the same date, but signed on January 30, 2009.

____

JUDGE PRESIDING

4

APPROVED AS TO FORM ONLY:

Law Firm for State of Texas
123 E. Legal Way
Austin, TX 78701
Tel: (512) 111-1111
Fax: (512) 222-2222

By:____________________________________
Attorney
State Bar No. 00000000
Attorney for State of Texas

Private Law Firm
246 W. 4th Street
Austin, TX 78701
Tel: (512) 333-3333
Fax: (512) 444-4444

By:____________________________________
Another Attorney
State Bar No. 1111111
Attorney for Mother

Another Private Law Firm
246 W. 5th Street
Austin, TX 78701
Tel: (512) 343-3333
Fax: (512) 454-4444

By:____________________________________
Yet Another Attorney
State Bar No. 22222222
Attorney for Father

____
Child's Attorney, Attorney Ad Litem

5

Appendix B: Final Decree of Divorce

THIS IS A <u>SAMPLE</u> DIVORCE DECREE, BUT IT IS FAIRLY TYPICAL IN MANY RESPECTS.

NO. <u>D-1-FM-10-01234</u>

IN THE MATTER OF	**§**	**IN THE DISTRICT COURT**
THE MARRIAGE OF	**§**	
	§	
MOTHER	**§**	
AND	**§**	**100TH JUDICIAL DISTRICT**
FATHER	**§**	
	§	
AND IN THE INTEREST OF	**§**	
OLDEST CHILD AND YOUNGEST CHILD, CHILDREN	**§**	**TRAVIS COUNTY, TEXAS**

This is the "style" of the case, identifying the parties, case number, and court. Every court pleading has a style.

FINAL DECREE OF DIVORCE

If these parents were not married, this custody order would be called "ORDER IN SUIT AFFECTING PARENT-CHILD RELATIONSHIP."

On January 25, 2010 the Court heard this case.

Appearances

Petitioner, Mother, appeared in person and through attorney of record, Smart Attorney, and announced ready for trial.

Respondent, Father, appeared in person and through attorney of record, Smart Lawyer, and announced ready for trial.

See last page for attorney contact info.

Record

The record of testimony was duly reported by the court reporter for the 100th Judicial District Court.

Jurisdiction and Domicile

The Court finds that the pleadings of Petitioner are in due form and contain all the allegations, information, and prerequisites required by law. The Court, after receiving evidence, finds that it has jurisdiction of this case and of all the parties and that at least sixty days have elapsed since the date the suit was filed. The Court finds that, at the time this suit was filed, Petitioner had been a domiciliary of Texas for the preceding six-month

Legal requirements for the court. Fortunately, none of your concern...

1

period and a resident of the county in which this suit was filed for the preceding ninety-day period. All persons entitled to citation were properly cited.

Jury

Jury trials are rare in these cases. →

A jury was waived, and questions of fact and of law were submitted to the Court.

Divorce

The D-I-V-O-R-C-E is FINAL. →

IT IS ORDERED AND DECREED that Mother, Petitioner, and Father, Respondent, are divorced and that the marriage between them is dissolved on the ground of insupportability.

But wait — there's more!!

CHILDREN →

Children of the Marriage

The Court finds that Petitioner and Respondent are the parents of the following children:

Children are identified.

Name: Oldest Child

Sex: Female

Birth date: January 1, 2003

Home state: Texas

Social Security number: XXX-XX-1234

Driver's license number and issuing state: n/a

Name: Youngest Child

Sex: Male

Birth date: January 1, 2004

Home state: Texas

Social Security number: XXX-XX-2345

Driver's license number and issuing state: n/a

2

Recall, there are 3 parts of an order dealing with children: (1) conservatorship, (2) possession and access, (3) child support. (See chapter 1.)

The Court finds no other children of the marriage are expected.

Parenting Plan

The Court finds that the provisions in this decree relating to the rights and duties of the parties with relation to the children, possession of and access to the children, child support, and optimizing the development of a close and continuing relationship between each party and the children constitute the parenting plan established by the Court.

IMPORTANT: We start with conservatorship. This is where decision-making rights are established.

Conservatorship

The Court, having considered the circumstances of the parents and of the children, finds that the following orders are in the best interest of the children.

IT IS ORDERED that Mother and Father are appointed Joint Managing Conservators of the following children: Oldest Child and Youngest Child.

Mom and Dad are JMCs. Does this mean their rights are equal? Not necessarily...

IT IS ORDERED that, at all times, Mother, as a parent joint managing conservator, shall have the following rights:

Here we see Mother's rights "at all times."

1. **the right to receive information from any other conservator of the children concerning the health, education, and welfare of the children;**

2. **the right to confer with the other parent to the extent possible before making a decision concerning the health, education, and welfare of the children;**

3. **the right of access to medical, dental, psychological, and educational records of the children;**

4. the right to consult with a physician, dentist, or psychologist of the children;

5. **the right to consult with school officials concerning the children's welfare and educational status, including school activities;**

6. **the right to attend school activities;**

7. the right to be designated on the children's records as a person to be notified in case of an emergency;

Note: We put educational rights in bold for your benefit. They won't be in bold in the orders you review.

3

Remember—
There are 3 parts to conservatorship rights:
(1) rights at all times, (2) rights during possession and access, (3) THE BIG RIGHTS!!

8. the right to consent to medical, dental, and surgical treatment during an emergency involving an immediate danger to the health and safety of the children; and

9. the right to manage the estates of the children to the extent the estates have been created by the parent or the parent's family.

Father's rights at all times...

IT IS ORDERED that, at all times, Father, as a parent joint managing conservator, shall have the following rights:

1. **the right to receive information from any other conservator of the children concerning the health, education, and welfare of the children;**

2. **the right to confer with the other parent to the extent possible before making a decision concerning the health, education, and welfare of the children;**

3. **the right of access to medical, dental, psychological, and educational records of the children;**

Whoa! This is a little different from Mother's rights. Also note: no right is listed to attend school activities!

4. the right to consult with a physician, dentist, or psychologist of the children;

5. **the right to consult with school officials via telephone or written communication concerning the children's welfare and educational status, including school activities;**

6. the right to be designated on the children's records as a person to be notified in case of an emergency;

7. the right to consent to medical, dental, and surgical treatment during an emergency involving an immediate danger to the health and safety of the children; and

9. the right to manage the estates of the children to the extent the estates have been created by the parent or the parent's family.

Note: There is an injunction against Father on pp. 35-36.

IT IS ORDERED that, at all times, Mother and Father, as parent joint managing

conservators, shall each have the following duties:

1. **the duty to inform the other conservator of the children in a timely manner of significant information concerning the health, education, and welfare of the children; and**

2. the duty to inform the other conservator of the children if the conservator resides with for at least thirty days, marries, or intends to marry a person who the conservator knows is registered as a sex offender under chapter 62 of the Code of Criminal Procedure or is currently charged with an offense for which on conviction the person would be required to register under that chapter. IT IS ORDERED that this information shall be tendered in the form of a notice made as soon as practicable, but not later than the fortieth day after the date the conservator of the children begins to reside with the person or on the tenth day after the date the marriage occurs, as appropriate. IT IS ORDERED that the notice must include a description of the offense that is the basis of the person's requirement to register as a sex offender or of the offense with which the person is charged. WARNING: A CONSERVATOR COMMITS AN OFFENSE PUNISHABLE AS A CLASS C MISDEMEANOR IF THE CONSERVATOR FAILS TO PROVIDE THIS NOTICE.

The 2nd part of conservatorship: rights during possession

IT IS ORDERED that, during their periods of possession, Mother and Father, as parent joint managing conservators, shall have the following rights and duties:

1. the duty of care, control, protection, and reasonable discipline of the children;

2. the duty to support the children, including providing the children with clothing, food, shelter, and medical and dental care not involving an invasive procedure;

3. the right to consent for the children to medical and dental care not involving an invasive procedure; and

4. the right to direct the moral and religious training of the children.

The 3rd part of conservatorship: THE BIG RIGHTS!

(Yeah, we know it doesn't say BIG RIGHTS, but these are the BIG RIGHTS.)

IT IS ORDERED that Mother, as a parent joint managing conservator, shall have the following rights and duty:

1. the exclusive right to designate the primary residence of the children within Travis County Texas and counties contiguous to Travis County, Texas.;

2. **the exclusive right to attend school activities;**

3. the exclusive right to consent to medical, dental, and surgical treatment involving invasive procedures;

4. the exclusive right to consent to psychiatric and psychological treatment of the children;

5. the exclusive right to receive and give receipt for periodic payments for

BIG RIGHTS continued

5

Observe Mother's exclusive right to attend school activities. Certainly this is related to the injunction against Father on pp. 35-36. What do you do if Father shows up at a school activity? See Chapter 4.

the support of the children and to hold or disburse these funds for the benefit of the children;

6. the exclusive right to represent the children in legal action and to make other decisions of substantial legal significance concerning the children;

7. the exclusive right to consent to marriage and to enlistment in the armed forces of the United States;

THIS IS THE BIG EDUCATION RIGHT YOU ARE LOOKING FOR. In this case, Mother owns it.

8. **the exclusive right to make decisions concerning the children's education;**

9. except as provided by section 264.0111 of the Texas Family Code, the exclusive right to the services and earnings of the children;

10. except when a guardian of the children's estates or a guardian or attorney ad litem has been appointed for the children, the exclusive right to act as an agent of the children in relation to the children's estates if the children's action is required by a state, the United States, or a foreign government; and

11. the exclusive duty to manage the estates of the children to the extent the estates have been created by community property or the joint property of the parent.

Father is a joint managing conservator, but he has NO BIG RIGHTS!

The Court finds that, in accordance with section 153.001 of the Texas Family Code, it is the public policy of Texas to assure that children will have frequent and continuing contact with parents who have shown the ability to act in the best interest of the child, to provide a safe, stable, and nonviolent environment for the child, and to encourage parents to share in the rights and duties of raising their child after the parents have separated or dissolved their marriage. IT IS ORDERED that the primary residence of the children shall be Travis County Texas and counties contiguous to Travis County, Texas., and the parties shall not remove the children from Travis County Texas and counties contiguous to Travis County, Texas. for the purpose of changing the primary residence of the children until modified by further order of the court of continuing jurisdiction or by written agreement signed by the parties and filed with the court. IT IS

6

You will deal with Mother for all educational decisions. What if educational decisions are to be shared, and Mother and Father disagree? See chapter 6.

FURTHER ORDERED that Mother shall have the exclusive right to designate the children's primary residence within Travis County Texas and counties contiguous to Travis County, Texas. IT IS ORDERED that this geographical restriction on the residence of the children shall be lifted if, at the time Mother wishes to remove the children from Travis County Texas and counties contiguous to Travis County, Texas for the purpose of changing the primary residence of the children, Father does not reside in Travis County Texas and counties contiguous to Travis County, Texas.

IT IS ORDERED that if a parent's consent is required for the issuance of a passport, that parent shall provide that consent in writing no later than ten days after receipt of the consent documents, unless the parent has good cause for withholding that consent.

IT IS ORDERED that either parent shall have the right to maintain possession of any passports of the children, Oldest Child and Youngest Child, subject to the requirements for delivery of the passports and all other requirements set forth below.

Either parent is ORDERED to deliver or cause to be delivered to the other parent the original, valid passports of Oldest Child and Youngest Child, within ten days of their receipt of the other parent's notice of intent to have the children travel outside the United States during a period of possession of the other parent.

IT IS ORDERED that if a conservator intends to have the children travel outside the United States during the conservator's period of possession of the children, the conservator shall provide written notice to the other conservator. IT IS ORDERED that this written notice shall include all the following:

1. any written consent form for travel outside the United States that is

7

required by the country of destination, countries through which travel will occur, or the intended carriers;

2. the date, time, and location of the children's departure from the United States;

3. a reasonable description of means of transportation, including, if applicable, all names of carriers, flight numbers, and scheduled departure and arrival times;

4. a reasonable description of each destination of the intended travel, including the name, address, and phone number of each interim destination and the final travel location;

5. the dates the children are scheduled to arrive and depart at each such destination;

6. the date, time, and location of the children's return to the United States;

7. a complete statement of each portion of the intended travel during which the conservator providing the written notice will not accompany the children; and

8. the name, permanent and mailing addresses, and work and home telephone numbers of each person accompanying the children on the intended travel other than the conservator providing the written notice.

This pertains to school travel.

If the intended travel is a group trip, such as with a school or other organization, the conservator providing the written notice is ORDERED to provide with the written notice all information about the group trip and its sponsor instead of stating the name, permanent and mailing addresses, and work and home telephone numbers of each person accompanying the children.

Remember, there are 3 parts of an order dealing with children: (1) conservatorship, (2) possession and access, (3) child support. (See chapter 1.)

IT IS FURTHER ORDERED that this written notice shall be furnished to the other conservator no less than twenty-one days before the intended day of departure of the children from the United States.

Mother and Father are each ORDERED to properly execute the written consent form to travel abroad and any other form required for the travel by the United States Department of State, passport authorities, foreign nations, travel organizers, school officials, or public carriers; when applicable, to have the forms duly notarized; and, within ten days of that conservator's receipt of each consent form, to deliver the form to the conservator providing the written notice.

IT IS ORDERED that any conservator who violates the terms and conditions of these provisions regarding the children's passports shall be liable for all costs incurred due to that person's noncompliance with these provisions. These costs shall include, but not be limited to, the expense of nonrefundable or noncreditable tickets, the costs of nonrefundable deposits for travel or lodging, attorney's fees, and all other costs incurred seeking enforcement of any of these provisions.

Here we see possession and access.

This section will tell you who delivers the kids to school and picks them up, and when.

Possession and Access

1. *Standard Possession Order*

The Court finds that the following provisions of this Standard Possession Order are intended to and do comply with the requirements of Texas Family Code sections 153.311 through 153.317. IT IS ORDERED that each conservator shall comply with all terms and conditions of this Standard Possession Order. IT IS ORDERED that this Standard Possession Order is effective immediately and applies to all periods of possession occurring on and after the date the Court signs this Standard Possession Order. IT IS, THEREFORE, ORDERED:

(a) Definitions

1. In this Standard Possession Order "school" means

the primary or secondary school in which the child is enrolled or, if the child is not enrolled in a primary or secondary school, the public school district in which the child primarily resides.

This is tricky, because it allows the parents to agree to times of possession outside of the order.

Should you get that agreement in writing before you release a child contrary to the terms of the order? See chapter 5 for discussion.

2. In this Standard Possession Order "child" includes each child, whether one or more, who is a subject of this suit while that child is under the age of eighteen years and not otherwise emancipated.

(b) Mutual Agreement or Specified Terms for Possession

IT IS ORDERED that the conservators shall have possession of the child at times mutually agreed to in advance by the parties, and, in the absence of mutual agreement, it is ORDERED that the conservators shall have possession of the child under the specified terms set out in this Standard Possession Order.

(c) Parents Who Reside 100 Miles or Less Apart

Except as otherwise explicitly provided in this Standard Possession Order, when Father resides 100 miles or less from the primary residence of the child, Father shall have the right to possession of the child as follows:

1. Weekends -

Father picks up child on 1st, 3rd, and 5th Fridays.

On weekends that occur during the regular school term, **beginning at the time the child's school is regularly dismissed**, on the first, third, and fifth Friday of each month and **ending at the time the child's school resumes after the weekend.**

On weekends that do not occur during the regular school term, beginning at 6:00 p.m., on the first, third, and fifth Friday of each month and ending at 6:00 p.m. on the following Sunday.

2. Weekend Possession Extended by a Holiday - Except as otherwise explicitly provided in this Standard Possession Order, **if a weekend period of possession by Father begins on a Friday that is a student holiday or teacher in-service day during the regular school term, as determined by the school in which the child is enrolled,** or a federal, state, or local holiday during the summer months when school is not in session, **or if the period ends on or is immediately followed by a Monday that is such a holiday, that weekend period of possession shall begin at the time the child's school is regularly dismissed on the Thursday immediately preceding the Friday holiday, student holiday or teacher in-service day** or end at 6:00 p.m. on that Monday holiday,

10

student holiday or teacher in-service day, as applicable.

3. Thursdays - On Thursday of each week during the regular school term, **beginning at the time the child's school is regularly dismissed** and ending at the time the child's school resumes on Friday.

This used to be Wednesdays in the standard Texas order, but was changed to thursdays.

4. Spring Break in Even-Numbered Years - In even-numbered years, **beginning at the time the child's school is regularly dismissed** on the day the child is dismissed from school for the school's spring vacation and ending at 6:00 p.m. on the day before school resumes after that vacation.

Spring break!

5. Extended Summer Possession by Father -

With Written Notice by April 1 - If Father gives Mother written notice by April 1 of a year specifying an extended period or periods of summer possession for that year, Father shall have possession of the child for thirty days beginning no earlier than the day after the child's school is dismissed for the summer vacation and ending no later than seven days before school resumes at the end of the summer vacation in that year, to be exercised in no more than two separate periods of at least seven consecutive days each, with each period of possession beginning and ending at 6:00 p.m on each applicable day, as specified in the written notice. These periods of possession shall begin and end at 6:00 p.m.

Without Written Notice by April 1 - If Father does not give Mother written notice by April 1 of a year specifying an extended period or periods of summer possession for that year, Father shall have possession of the child for thirty consecutive days in that year beginning at 6:00 p.m. on July 1 and ending at 6:00 p.m. on July 31.

Notwithstanding the Thursday periods of possession during the regular school term and the weekend periods of possession ORDERED for Father, it is explicitly ORDERED that Mother shall have a superior right of possession of the child as follows:

1. Spring Break in Odd-Numbered Years - In odd-numbered years, beginning at the time the child's school is regularly dismissed on the day the child is dismissed from school for the school's spring vacation and ending at 6:00 p.m. on the day before school resumes after that vacation.

2. Summer Weekend Possession by Mother - If Mother gives Father written notice by April 15 of a year, Mother shall have

11

possession of the child on any one weekend beginning at 6:00 p.m. on Friday and ending at 6:00 p.m. on the following Sunday during any one period of the extended summer possession by Father in that year, provided that Mother picks up the child from Father and returns the child to that same place and that the weekend so designated does not interfere with Father's Day Weekend.

3. Extended Summer Possession by Mother - If Mother gives Father written notice by April 15 of a year or gives Father fourteen days' written notice on or after April 16 of a year, Mother may designate one weekend beginning no earlier than the day after the child's school is dismissed for the summer vacation and ending no later than seven days before school resumes at the end of the summer vacation, during which an otherwise scheduled weekend period of possession by Father shall not take place in that year, provided that the weekend so designated does not interfere with Father's period or periods of extended summer possession or with Father's Day Weekend.

This should be self-evident. If it's not, consult a map. →

(d) Parents Who Reside More Than 100 Miles Apart

Except as otherwise explicitly provided in this Standard Possession Order, when Father resides more than 100 miles from the residence of the child, Father shall have the right to possession of the child as follows:

Weekends

1. Weekends - Unless Father elects the alternative period of weekend possession described in the next paragraph, Father shall have the right to possession of the child on weekends that occur during the regular school term, **beginning at the time school is dismissed**, on the first, third, and fifth Friday of each month and ending at 6:00 p.m. on the following Sunday, and on weekends that do not occur during the regular school term, beginning at 6:00 p.m. on the first, third and fifth Friday of each month and ending at 6:00 p.m. on the following Sunday. Except as otherwise explicitly provided in this Standard Possession Order, **if such a weekend period of possession by Father begins on a Friday that is a student holiday or teacher in-service day during the regular school term, as determined by the school in which the child is enrolled,** or a federal, state, or local holiday during the summer months when school is not in session, **or if the period ends on or is immediately followed by a Monday that is such a holiday, that weekend period of possession shall begin at the time the child's school is regularly dismissed on the Thursday immediately preceding the Friday holiday, student holiday or teacher in-service day** or end at 6:00 p.m. on that Monday holiday, student holiday or teacher in-service day, as applicable.

12

Alternate Weekend Possession - In lieu of the weekend possession described in the foregoing paragraph, Father shall have the right to possession of the child not more than one weekend per month of Father's choice beginning at 6:00 p.m. on the day school recesses for the weekend and ending at 6:00 p.m. on the day before school resumes after the weekend. Except as otherwise explicitly provided in this Standard Possession Order, if such a weekend period of possession by Father begins on a Friday that is a student holiday or teacher in-service day during the regular school term, as determined by the school in which the child is enrolled, or a federal, state, or local holiday during the summer months when school is not in session, or if the period ends on or is immediately followed by a Monday that is such a holiday, **that weekend period of possession shall begin at the time the child's school is regularly dismissed on the Thursday immediately preceding the Friday holiday, student holiday or teacher in-service day** or end at 6:00 p.m. on that Monday holiday, student holiday or teacher in-service day, as applicable. Father may elect an option for this alternative period of weekend possession by giving written notice to Mother within ninety days after the parties begin to reside more than 100 miles apart. If Father makes this election, Father shall give Mother fourteen days' written or telephonic notice preceding a designated weekend. The weekends chosen shall not conflict with the provisions regarding Christmas, Thanksgiving, the child's birthday, and Mother's Day Weekend below.

2. Spring Break in All Years - Every year, beginning at 6:00 p.m. on the day the child is dismissed from school for the school's spring vacation and ending at 6:00 p.m. on the day before school resumes after that vacation.

3. Extended Summer Possession by Father -

With Written Notice by April 1 - If Father gives Mother written notice by April 1 of a year specifying an extended period or periods of summer possession for that year, Father shall have possession of the child for forty-two days beginning no earlier than the day after the child's school is dismissed for the summer vacation and ending no later than seven days before school resumes at the end of the summer vacation in that year, to be exercised in no more than two separate periods of at least seven consecutive days each, with each period of possession beginning and ending at 6:00 p.m. on each applicable day, as specified in the written notice. These periods of possession shall begin and end at 6:00 p.m.

Without Written Notice by April 1 - If Father does not give Mother written notice by April 1 of a year specifying an extended period

13

or periods of summer possession for that year, Father shall have possession of the child for forty-two consecutive days beginning at 6:00 p.m. on June 15 and ending at 6:00 p.m. on July 27 of that year.

Notwithstanding the weekend periods of possession ORDERED for Father, it is explicitly ORDERED that Mother shall have a superior right of possession of the child as follows:

1. Summer Weekend Possession by Mother - If Mother gives Father written notice by April 15 of a year, Mother shall have possession of the child on any one weekend beginning at 6:00 p.m. on Friday and ending at 6:00 p.m. on the following Sunday during any one period of possession by Father during Father's extended summer possession in that year, provided that if a period of possession by Father in that year exceeds thirty days, Mother may have possession of the child under the terms of this provision on any two nonconsecutive weekends during that period and provided that Mother picks up the child from Father and returns the child to that same place and that the weekend so designated does not interfere with Father's Day Weekend.

2. Extended Summer Possession by Mother - If Mother gives Father written notice by April 15 of a year, Mother may designate twenty-one days beginning no earlier than the day after the child's school is dismissed for the summer vacation and ending no later than seven days before school resumes at the end of the summer vacation in that year, to be exercised in no more than two separate periods of at least seven consecutive days each, with each period of possession beginning and ending at 6:00 p.m. on each applicable day, during which Father shall not have possession of the child, provided that the period or periods so designated do not interfere with Father's period or periods of extended summer possession or with Father's Day Weekend.

(e) Holidays Unaffected by Distance

Notwithstanding the weekend and Thursday periods of possession of Father, Mother and Father shall have the right to possession of the child as follows:

Christmas

1. Christmas Holidays in Even-Numbered Years - In even-numbered years, Father shall have the right to possession of the child **beginning at the time the child's school is regularly dismissed on the day the child is dismissed from school for the Christmas school vacation** and ending at noon on December 28, and Mother shall have the right to possession of the child beginning at noon on December 28 and ending at 6:00 p.m. on the day before school resumes after that

Christmas school vacation.

2. Christmas Holidays in Odd-Numbered Years - In odd-numbered years, Mother shall have the right to possession of the child **beginning at the time the child's school is regularly dismissed on the day the child is dismissed from school for the Christmas school vacation** and ending at noon on December 28, and Father shall have the right to possession of the child beginning at noon on December 28 and ending at 6:00 p.m. on the day before school resumes after that Christmas school vacation.

3. Thanksgiving in Odd-Numbered Years - In odd-numbered years, Father shall have the right to possession of the child **beginning at the time the child's school is regularly dismissed on the day the child is dismissed from school for the Thanksgiving holiday** and ending at 6:00 p.m. on the Sunday following Thanksgiving.

Thanksgiving

4. Thanksgiving in Even-Numbered Years - In even-numbered years, Mother shall have the right to possession of the child **beginning at the time the child's school is regularly dismissed on the day the child is dismissed from school for the Thanksgiving holiday** and ending at 6:00 p.m. on the Sunday following Thanksgiving.

5. Child's Birthday - If a parent is not otherwise entitled under this Standard Possession Order to present possession of a child on the child's birthday, that parent shall have possession of the child and the child's minor siblings beginning at 6:00 p.m. and ending at 8:00 p.m. on that day, provided that that parent picks up the children from the other parent's residence and returns the children to that same place.

Birthdays

6. Father's Day Weekend - Father shall have the right to possession of the child each year, beginning at 6:00 p.m. on the Friday preceding Father's Day and ending at 6:00 p.m. on Father's Day, provided that if Father is not otherwise entitled under this Standard Possession Order to present possession of the child, he shall pick up the child from Mother's residence and return the child to that same place.

Father's Day

7. Mother's Day Weekend - Mother shall have the right to possession of the child each year, beginning at the time the child's school is regularly dismissed on the Friday preceding Mother's Day and ending at the time the child's school resumes after Mother's Day, provided that if Mother is not otherwise entitled under this Standard Possession Order to present possession of the child, she shall pick up the child from Father's residence and return the child to that same place.

Mother's Day

(f) Undesignated Periods of Possession

Mother shall have the **right of possession of the child at all other times not specifically designated in this Standard Possession Order for Father.**

(g) General Terms and Conditions

Except as otherwise explicitly provided in this Standard Possession Order, the terms and conditions of possession of the child that apply regardless of the distance between the residence of a parent and the child are as follows:

1. Surrender of Child by Mother - Mother is ORDERED to surrender the child to Father at the beginning of each period of Father's possession at the residence of Mother.

School is commonly the point of surrender.

If a period of possession by Father begins at the time the child's school is regularly dismissed, Mother is ORDERED to surrender the child to Father at the beginning of each such period of possession at the school in which the child is enrolled. If the child is not in school, Father shall pick up the child at the residence of Mother at 6:00 p.m., and Mother is ORDERED to surrender the child to Father at the residence of Mother at 6:00 p.m. under these circumstances.

2. Surrender of Child by Father - Father is ORDERED to surrender the child to Mother at the residence of Father at the end of each period of possession.

If a period of possession by Father ends at the time the child's school resumes, Father is ORDERED to surrender the child to Mother at the end of each such period of possession at the school in which the child is enrolled or, if the child is not in school, at the residence of Mother at 6:00 p.m.

3. Surrender of Child by Father - Father is ORDERED to surrender the child to Mother, if the child is in Father's possession or subject to Father's control, at the beginning of each period of Mother's exclusive periods of possession, at the place designated in this Standard Possession Order.

4. Return of Child by Mother - Mother is ORDERED to return the child to Father, if Father is entitled to possession of the child, at the end of each of Mother's exclusive periods of possession, at the place designated in this Standard Possession Order.

16

5. Personal Effects - Each conservator is ORDERED to return with the child the personal effects that the child brought at the beginning of the period of possession.

6. Designation of Competent Adult - Each conservator may designate any competent adult to pick up and return the child, as applicable. IT IS ORDERED that a conservator or a designated competent adult be present when the child is picked up or returned.

7. Inability to Exercise Possession - Each conservator is ORDERED to give notice to the person in possession of the child on each occasion that the conservator will be unable to exercise that conservator's right of possession for any specified period.

8. Written Notice - Written notice shall be deemed to have been timely made if received or postmarked before or at the time that notice is due.

9. **Notice to School and Mother - If Father's time of possession of the child ends at the time school resumes and for any reason the child is not or will not be returned to school, Father shall immediately notify the school and Mother that the child will not be or has not been returned to school.**

> School should be notified if child is not returned to school.

This concludes the Standard Possession Order.

2. *Duration*

The periods of possession ordered above apply to each child the subject of this suit while that child is under the age of eighteen years and not otherwise emancipated.

3. *Termination of Orders*

The provisions of this decree relating to conservatorship, possession, or access terminate on the remarriage of Mother to Father unless a nonparent or agency has been appointed conservator of the children under chapter 153 of the Texas Family Code.

17

The third part of the order concerns child support.

This should have little impact on the school, if any. Unless otherwise intrigued, you may skip to page 28.

Child Support

IT IS ORDERED that Father is obligated to pay and shall pay to Mother child support of $1,200 per month, with the first payment being due and payable on February 1, 2010 and a like payment being due and payable on the first day of each month thereafter until the first month following the date of the earliest occurrence of one of the events specified below:

1. any child reaches the age of eighteen years or graduates from high school, whichever occurs later, subject to the provisions for support beyond the age of eighteen years set out below;

2. any child marries;

3. any child dies;

4. the child enlists in the armed forces of the United States and begins active service as defined by section 101 of title 10 of the United States Code; or

5. any child's disabilities are otherwise removed for general purposes; or

Thereafter, Father is ORDERED to pay to Mother child support of $960 per month, due and payable on the first day of the first month immediately following the date of the earliest occurrence of one of the events specified above for the other child and a like sum of $960 due and payable on the first day of each month thereafter until the next occurrence of one of the events specified above for the other child.

If the child is eighteen years of age and has not graduated from high school, IT IS ORDERED that Father's obligation to pay child support to Mother shall not terminate but shall continue for as long as the child is enrolled-

1. under chapter 25 of the Texas Education Code in an accredited

secondary school in a program leading toward a high school diploma or under section 130.008 of the Education Code in courses for joint high school and junior college credit and is complying with the minimum attendance requirements of subchapter C of chapter 25 of the Education Code or

2. on a full-time basis in a private secondary school in a program leading toward a high school diploma and is complying with the minimum attendance requirements imposed by that school.

Statement on Guidelines

In accordance with Texas Family Code section 154.130, the Court makes the following findings and conclusions regarding the child support order made in open court in this case on January 25, 2010:

1. the amount of child support ordered by the Court is in accordance with the percentage guidelines;

2. the amount of net resources available to Father per month is $4,800;

3. the amount of net resources available to Mother per month is $2,700; and

4. the percentage applied to Father's net resources for child support is 25 percent.

Withholding from Earnings

IT IS ORDERED that any employer of Father shall be ordered to withhold from earnings for child support from the disposable earnings of Father for the support of Oldest Child and Youngest Child.

IT IS FURTHER ORDERED that all amounts withheld from the disposable earnings of Father by the employer and paid in accordance with the order to that employer shall constitute a credit against the child support obligation. Payment of the full amount of child support ordered paid by this decree through the means of withholding from earnings shall discharge the child support obligation. If the amount withheld from earnings and credited against the child support obligation is less than 100 percent of the amount ordered to be paid by this decree, the balance due remains an obligation of Father, and it is hereby ORDERED that Father pay the balance due directly to the state disbursement unit specified below.

On this date the Court signed an Order/Notice to Withhold Income for Child Support.

Payment

IT IS ORDERED that all payments shall be made through the state disbursement unit at Texas Child Support Disbursement Unit, P.O. Box 659791, San Antonio, Texas 78265-9791, and thereafter promptly remitted to Mother for the support of the children. IT IS ORDERED that each party shall pay, when due, all fees charged to that party by the state disbursement unit and any other agency statutorily authorized to charge a fee.

Change of Employment

IT IS FURTHER ORDERED that Father shall notify this Court and Mother by U.S. certified mail, return receipt requested, of any change of address and of any termination of employment. This notice shall be given no later than seven days after the change of address or the termination of employment. This notice or a subsequent notice shall also provide the current address of Father and the name and address of his current employer, whenever that information becomes available.

Clerk's Duties

IT IS ORDERED that, on the request of a prosecuting attorney, the title IV-D agency, the friend of the Court, a domestic relations office, Mother, Father, or an attorney representing Mother or Father, the clerk of this Court shall cause a certified copy of the Order/Notice to Withhold Income for Child Support to be delivered to any employer.

Health Care

1. IT IS ORDERED that Mother and Father shall each provide medical support for each child as set out in this order as additional child support for as long as the Court may order Mother and Father to provide support for the child under sections 154.001 and 154.002 of the Texas Family Code. Beginning on the day Mother and Father's actual or potential obligation to support a child under sections 154.001 and 154.002 of the Family Code terminates, IT IS ORDERED that Mother and Father are discharged from the obligations set forth in this medical support order with respect to that child, except for any failure by a parent to fully comply with those obligations before that date.

2. Definitions -

"Health Insurance" means insurance coverage that provides basic health-care services, including usual physician services, office visits, hospitalization, and laboratory, X-ray, and emergency services, that may be provided through a health maintenance organization or other private or public organization, other than medical assistance under chapter 32 of the Texas Human Resources Code.

"Reasonable cost" means the cost of health insurance coverage for a child that does not exceed 9 percent of the obligor's annual resources, as described by section 154.062(b) of the Texas Family Code, if the obligor is responsible under a medical support order for the cost of health insurance coverage for only one child. If the obligor is responsible under a medical support order for the cost of health insurance coverage for more than one child, "reasonable cost" means the total cost of health insurance coverage for all children for which the obligor is responsible under a medical support order that does not exceed 9 percent of the obligor's annual resources, as described by section 154.062(b) of the Texas Family Code.

"Reasonable and necessary health-care expenses not paid by insurance and incurred by or on behalf of a child" include, without limitation, any copayments for office visits or prescription drugs, the yearly deductible, if any, and medical, surgical, prescription drug, mental health-care services, dental, eye care, ophthalmological, and orthodontic charges. These reasonable and necessary health-care expenses do not include expenses for travel to and from the health-care provider or for nonprescription medication.

"Furnish" means:

a. to hand deliver the document by a person eighteen years of age or older either to the recipient or to a person who is eighteen years of age or older and permanently resides with the recipient;

b. to deliver the document to the recipient by certified mail, return receipt requested, to the recipient's last known mailing or residence address; or

c. to deliver the document to the recipient at the recipient's last known mailing or residence address using any person or entity whose principal business is that of a courier or deliverer of papers or documents either within or outside the United States.

3. Findings on Health Insurance Availability - IT IS FOUND:

Health insurance is available or is in effect for the children through Father's employment or membership in a union, trade association, or other organization at a reasonable cost of $150.

IT IS FURTHER FOUND that the following orders regarding health-care coverage are in the best interest of the children.

4. Provision of Health-Care Coverage -

As additional child support, Father is ORDERED to continue to maintain health insurance for each child who is the subject of this suit that covers basic health-care services, including usual physician services, office visits, hospitalization, laboratory, X-ray, and emergency services.

Father is ORDERED to maintain such health insurance in full force and effect on each child who is the subject of this suit as long as child support is payable for that child. Father is ORDERED to convert any group insurance to individual coverage or obtain other health insurance for each child within fifteen days of termination of his employment or other disqualification from the group insurance. Father is ORDERED to exercise any conversion options or acquisition of new health insurance in such a manner that the resulting insurance equals or exceeds that in effect immediately before the change.

Father is ORDERED to furnish Mother a true and correct copy of the health insurance policy or certification and a schedule of benefits within ten days of the signing of this order. Father is ORDERED to furnish Mother the insurance cards and any other

23

forms necessary for use of the insurance within ten days of the signing of this order. Father is ORDERED to provide, within three days of receipt by him, to Mother any insurance checks, other payments, or explanations of benefits relating to any medical expenses for the children that Mother paid or incurred.

Pursuant to section 1504.051 of the Texas Insurance Code, IT IS ORDERED that if Father is eligible for dependent health coverage but fails to apply to obtain coverage for the children, the insurer shall enroll the children on application of Mother or others as authorized by law.

Pursuant to section 154.183(c) of the Texas Family Code, the reasonable and necessary health-care expenses of the children that are not reimbursed by health insurance are allocated as follows: Mother is ORDERED to pay 50 percent and Father is ORDERED to pay 50 percent of the unreimbursed health-care expenses if, at the time the expenses are incurred, Father is providing health insurance as ordered.

The party who incurs a health-care expense on behalf of a child is ORDERED to submit to the other party all forms, receipts, bills, and statements reflecting the uninsured portion of the health-care expenses within thirty days after he or she receives them. The nonincurring party is ORDERED to pay his or her percentage of the uninsured portion of the health-care expenses either by paying the health care provider directly or by reimbursing the incurring party for any advance payment exceeding the incurring party's percentage of the uninsured portion of the health-care expenses within thirty days after the nonincurring party receives the forms, receipts, bills, or statements.

These provisions apply to all unreimbursed health-care expenses of any child who is the subject of this suit that are incurred while child support is payable for that child.

5. Secondary Coverage - IT IS ORDERED that if a party provides secondary health insurance coverage for the children, both parties shall cooperate fully with regard to the handling and filing of claims with the insurance carrier providing the coverage in order to maximize the benefits available to the children and to ensure that the party who pays for health-care expenses for the children is reimbursed for the payment from both carriers to the fullest extent possible.

6. Compliance with Insurance Company Requirements - Each party is ORDERED to conform to all requirements imposed by the terms and conditions of the policy of health insurance covering the children in order to assure maximum reimbursement or direct payment by the insurance company of the incurred health-care expense, including but not limited to requirements for advance notice to any carrier, second opinions, and the like. Each party is ORDERED to attempt to use "preferred providers," or services within the health maintenance organization, if applicable; however, this provision shall not apply if emergency care is required. Disallowance of the bill by a health insurer shall not excuse the obligation of either party to make payment; however, if a bill is disallowed or the benefit reduced because of the failure of a party to follow insurance procedures or requirements, IT IS ORDERED that the party failing to follow the insurance procedures or requirements shall be wholly responsible for the increased portion of that bill.

7. Claims - Except as provided in this paragraph, the party who is not carrying the health insurance policy covering the children is ORDERED to furnish to the party carrying the policy, within fifteen days of receiving them, any and all forms,

receipts, bills, and statements reflecting the health-care expenses the party not carrying the policy incurs on behalf of the children. In accordance with section 1204.251 and 1504.055(a) of the Texas Insurance Code, IT IS ORDERED that the party who is not carrying the health insurance policy covering the children, at that party's option or others as authorized by law, may file any claims for health-care expenses directly with the insurance carrier with and from whom coverage is provided for the benefit of the children and receive payments directly from the insurance company. Further, for the sole purpose of section 1204.251 of the Texas Insurance Code, Mother is designated the managing conservator or possessory conservator of the children.

The party who is carrying the health insurance policy covering the children is ORDERED to submit all forms required by the insurance company for payment or reimbursement of health-care expenses incurred by either party on behalf of a child to the insurance carrier within fifteen days of that party's receiving any form, receipt, bill, or statement reflecting the expenses.

8. Constructive Trust for Payments Received - IT IS ORDERED that any insurance payments received by a party from the health insurance carrier as reimbursement for health-care expenses incurred by or on behalf of a child shall belong to the party who paid those expenses. IT IS FURTHER ORDERED that the party receiving the insurance payments is designated a constructive trustee to receive any insurance checks or payments for health-care expenses paid by the other party, and the party carrying the policy shall endorse and forward the checks or payments, along with any explanation of benefits received, to the other party within three days of receiving them.

9. WARNING - A PARENT ORDERED TO PROVIDE HEALTH INSURANCE OR TO PAY THE OTHER PARENT ADDITIONAL CHILD SUPPORT FOR THE COST OF HEALTH INSURANCE WHO FAILS TO DO SO IS LIABLE FOR NECESSARY MEDICAL EXPENSES OF THE CHILDREN, WITHOUT REGARD TO WHETHER THE EXPENSES WOULD HAVE BEEN PAID IF HEALTH INSURANCE HAD BEEN PROVIDED, AND FOR THE COST OF HEALTH INSURANCE PREMIUMS OR CONTRIBUTIONS, IF ANY, PAID ON BEHALF OF THE CHILDREN.

Miscellaneous Child Support Provisions

No Credit for Informal Payments

IT IS ORDERED that the child support as prescribed in this decree shall be exclusively discharged in the manner ordered and that any direct payments made by Father to Mother or any expenditures incurred by Father during Father's periods of possession of or access to the children, as prescribed in this decree, for food, clothing, gifts, travel, shelter, or entertainment are deemed in addition to and not in lieu of the support ordered in this decree.

Support as Obligation of Estate

IT IS ORDERED that the provisions for child support in this decree shall be an obligation of the estate of Father and shall not terminate on the death of Father. Payments received for the benefit of the children, including payments from the Social Security Administration, Department of Veterans Affairs or other governmental agency or life insurance proceeds, annuity payments, trust distributions, or retirement survivor benefits, shall be a credit against this obligation. Any remaining balance of the child

27

support is an obligation of Father's estate.

Termination of Orders on Remarriage of Parties

The provisions of this decree relating to current child support terminate on the remarriage of Mother to Father unless a nonparent or agency has been appointed conservator of the children under chapter 153 of the Texas Family Code. An obligation to pay child support under this decree does not terminate on the death of Mother but continues as an obligation to Oldest Child and Youngest Child.

Settlement of Future Disputes

The Court finds that the parties agree to the following.

How will Mother and Father settle disputes?

Mediation

It is agreed that before setting any hearing or initiating discovery in a suit for modification of the terms and conditions of conservatorship, possession, or support of the children, except in an emergency, the parties shall mediate the controversy in good faith. This requirement does not apply to actions brought to enforce this Final Decree of Divorce or to enforce any subsequent modifications of this decree. It is agreed that the party wishing to modify the terms and conditions of conservatorship, possession, or support of the children shall give written notice to the other party of a desire to mediate the controversy. If, within ten days after receipt of the written notice, the parties cannot agree on a mediator or the other party does not agree to attend mediation or fails to attend a scheduled mediation of the controversy, the party desiring modification shall be released from the obligation to mediate and shall be free to file suit for modification.

Information Regarding Parties

The information required for each party by section 105.006(a) of the Texas Family Code is as follows:

Name: Mother

Social Security number: XXX-XX-3456

Driver's license number: 11111111 Issuing state: Texas

Current residence address: 1000 Sunshine Lane, Austin, Texas 78701

Mailing address: 1000 Sunshine Lane, Austin, Texas 78701

Home telephone number: 512/444-4444

Name of employer: State of Texas

Address of employment: 1111 Worker's Lane, Austin, TX 78701

Work telephone number: 512/222-2222

Name: Father

Social Security number: XXX-XX-4567

Driver's license number 22222222 Issuing state: Texas

Current residence address: 1000 Happy Drive, Austin, Texas 78701

Mailing address: 1000 Happy Drive, Austin, Texas 78701

Home telephone number: 512/333-3333

Name of employer: Johnson Company

Address of employment: 1111 Corporate Lane, Austin, TX 78701

Work telephone number: 512/555-5555

Mother and Father contact info.

EACH PERSON WHO IS A PARTY TO THIS ORDER IS ORDERED TO NOTIFY EACH OTHER PARTY, THE COURT, AND THE STATE CASE REGISTRY

29

OF ANY CHANGE IN THE PARTY'S CURRENT RESIDENCE ADDRESS, MAILING ADDRESS, HOME TELEPHONE NUMBER, NAME OF EMPLOYER, ADDRESS OF EMPLOYMENT, DRIVER'S LICENSE NUMBER, AND WORK TELEPHONE NUMBER. THE PARTY IS ORDERED TO GIVE NOTICE OF AN INTENDED CHANGE IN ANY OF THE REQUIRED INFORMATION TO EACH OTHER PARTY, THE COURT, AND THE STATE CASE REGISTRY ON OR BEFORE THE 6OTH DAY BEFORE THE INTENDED CHANGE. IF THE PARTY DOES NOT KNOW OR COULD NOT HAVE KNOWN OF THE CHANGE IN SUFFICIENT TIME TO PROVIDE 60-DAY NOTICE, THE PARTY IS ORDERED TO GIVE NOTICE OF THE CHANGE ON OR BEFORE THE FIFTH DAY AFTER THE DATE THAT THE PARTY KNOWS OF THE CHANGE.

THE DUTY TO FURNISH THIS INFORMATION TO EACH OTHER PARTY, THE COURT, AND THE STATE CASE REGISTRY CONTINUES AS LONG AS ANY PERSON, BY VIRTUE OF THIS ORDER, IS UNDER AN OBLIGATION TO PAY CHILD SUPPORT OR ENTITLED TO POSSESSION OF OR ACCESS TO A CHILD.

FAILURE BY A PARTY TO OBEY THE ORDER OF THIS COURT TO PROVIDE EACH OTHER PARTY, THE COURT, AND THE STATE CASE REGISTRY WITH THE CHANGE IN THE REQUIRED INFORMATION MAY RESULT IN FURTHER LITIGATION TO ENFORCE THE ORDER, INCLUDING CONTEMPT OF COURT. A FINDING OF CONTEMPT MAY BE PUNISHED BY CONFINEMENT IN JAIL FOR UP TO SIX MONTHS, A FINE OF UP TO $500 FOR EACH VIOLATION, AND A MONEY JUDGMENT FOR PAYMENT OF

ATTORNEY'S FEES AND COURT COSTS.

Notice shall be given to the other party by delivering a copy of the notice to the party by registered or certified mail, return receipt requested. Notice shall be given to the Court by delivering a copy of the notice either in person to the clerk of this Court or by registered or certified mail addressed to the clerk at the Travis County District Clerk's Office, P.O. Box 1495, Austin, TX 78767. Notice shall be given to the state case registry by mailing a copy of the notice to State Case Registry, Contract Services Section, MC046S, P.O. Box 12017, Austin, Texas 78711-2017.

NOTICE TO ANY PEACE OFFICER OF THE STATE OF TEXAS: **YOU MAY USE REASONABLE EFFORTS TO ENFORCE THE TERMS OF CHILD CUSTODY SPECIFIED IN THIS ORDER.** A PEACE OFFICER WHO RELIES ON THE TERMS OF A COURT ORDER AND THE OFFICER'S AGENCY ARE ENTITLED TO THE APPLICABLE IMMUNITY AGAINST ANY CLAIM, CIVIL OR OTHERWISE, REGARDING THE OFFICER'S GOOD FAITH ACTS PERFORMED IN THE SCOPE OF THE OFFICER'S DUTIES IN ENFORCING THE TERMS OF THE ORDER THAT RELATE TO CHILD CUSTODY. ANY PERSON WHO KNOWINGLY PRESENTS FOR ENFORCEMENT AN ORDER THAT IS INVALID OR NO LONGER IN EFFECT COMMITS AN OFFENSE THAT MAY BE PUNISHABLE BY CONFINEMENT IN JAIL FOR AS LONG AS TWO YEARS AND A FINE OF AS MUCH AS $10,000.

WARNINGS TO PARTIES: FAILURE TO OBEY A COURT ORDER FOR CHILD SUPPORT OR FOR POSSESSION OF OR ACCESS TO A CHILD MAY RESULT IN FURTHER LITIGATION TO ENFORCE THE ORDER, INCLUDING

CONTEMPT OF COURT. A FINDING OF CONTEMPT MAY BE PUNISHED BY CONFINEMENT IN JAIL FOR UP TO SIX MONTHS, A FINE OF UP TO $500 FOR EACH VIOLATION, AND A MONEY JUDGMENT FOR PAYMENT OF ATTORNEY'S FEES AND COURT COSTS.

FAILURE OF A PARTY TO MAKE A CHILD SUPPORT PAYMENT TO THE PLACE AND IN THE MANNER REQUIRED BY A COURT ORDER MAY RESULT IN THE PARTY'S NOT RECEIVING CREDIT FOR MAKING THE PAYMENT.

FAILURE OF A PARTY TO PAY CHILD SUPPORT DOES NOT JUSTIFY DENYING THAT PARTY COURT-ORDERED POSSESSION OF OR ACCESS TO A CHILD. REFUSAL BY A PARTY TO ALLOW POSSESSION OF OR ACCESS TO A CHILD DOES NOT JUSTIFY FAILURE TO PAY COURT-ORDERED CHILD SUPPORT TO THAT PARTY.

This is where marital property is split up. We spared you the details.

Division of Marital Estate

The Court finds that no community property other than personal effects has been accumulated by the parties.

IT IS ORDERED AND DECREED that the personal effects of the parties are awarded to the party having possession.

Division of Debt

Debts to Husband

IT IS ORDERED AND DECREED that the husband, Father, shall pay, as a part of the division of the estate of the parties, and shall indemnify and hold the wife and her property harmless from any failure to so discharge, these items:

32

H-1. All debts, charges, liabilities, and other obligations incurred solely by the husband from and after December 1, 2009 unless express provision is made in this decree to the contrary.

Debts to Wife

IT IS ORDERED AND DECREED that the wife, Mother, shall pay, as a part of the division of the estate of the parties, and shall indemnify and hold the husband and his property harmless from any failure to so discharge, these items:

W-1. All debts, charges, liabilities, and other obligations incurred solely by the wife from and after December 1, 2009 unless express provision is made in this decree to the contrary.

Notice

IT IS ORDERED AND DECREED that each party shall send to the other party, within three days of its receipt, a copy of any correspondence from a creditor or taxing authority concerning any potential liability of the other party.

Attorney's Fees

To effect an equitable division of the estate of the parties and as a part of the division, and for services rendered in connection with conservatorship and support of the children, each party shall be responsible for his or her own attorney's fees, expenses, and costs incurred as a result of legal representation in this case.

Treatment/Allocation of Community Income for Year of Divorce

IT IS ORDERED AND DECREED that, for the calendar year 2010, each party shall file an individual income tax return in accordance with the Internal Revenue Code and report as the party's income 50 percent of all predivorce community income or loss

33

attributable to the parties, all postdivorce income attributable to the reporting party, and all the reporting party's separate income during any part of the year. Each party shall take credit for 50 percent of all prior year overpayments, estimated tax payments, and withholdings occurring before the date of divorce and for 100 percent of the reporting party's estimated tax payments and withholdings occurring after the date of divorce.

IT IS ORDERED AND DECREED that, for the calendar year 2010, each party shall timely pay and indemnify and hold the other party and his or her property harmless from any federal income tax liability attributable to the personal earnings of the reporting party and any net income resulting from property subject to the sole management and control of the reporting party from January 1 of that year through the date of divorce and for all such postdivorce earnings and income.

IT IS ORDERED AND DECREED that each party shall be entitled to use as a credit against his or her tax liability all estimated tax payments, credit for tax payments made in prior years, and withholdings made solely in the name of the reporting party and 50 percent of such estimated tax payments, credit for tax payments, and withholdings made in the names of both parties before the date of divorce together with any net loss resulting from property subject to the sole management and control of the reporting party and 50 percent of any net loss attributable to property subject to the joint management of the parties.

IT IS ORDERED AND DECREED that for calendar year 2010, each party shall indemnify and hold the other party and his or her property harmless from any tax liability associated with the reporting party's individual tax return for that year unless the parties have agreed to allocate their tax liability in a manner different from that reflected on their

34

returns.

IT IS ORDERED AND DECREED that each party shall furnish such information to the other party as is requested to prepare federal income tax returns for 2010 within thirty days of receipt of a written request for the information, and in no event shall the available information be exchanged later than March 1, 2011. As requested information becomes available after that date, it shall be provided within ten days of receipt.

IT IS ORDERED AND DECREED that all payments made to the other party in accordance with the allocation provisions for payment of federal income taxes contained in this Final Decree of Divorce are not deemed income to the party receiving those payments but are part of the property division and necessary for a just and right division of the parties' estate.

Permanent Injunctions as to Persons

THIS IS AN IMPORTANT PART. It is not common, but certainly possible.

The Court finds that, because of the conduct of Father, a permanent injunction against him should be granted as appropriate relief because there is no adequate remedy at law.

The permanent injunction granted below shall be effective immediately and shall be binding on Father; on his agents, servants, employees, and attorneys; and on those persons in active concert or participation with them who receive actual notice of this order by personal service or otherwise.

IT IS ORDERED AND DECREED that Father is permanently enjoined from:

1. Causing physical contact or bodily injury to Mother or threatening Mother with imminent bodily injury.

35

2. Communicating in person, by telephone, or in writing with Mother, except for arranging visitation or notifying Mother of circumstances affecting the best interest of the children.

3. Coming within 200 yards of, entering, or remaining on the premises of the residence of Mother, located at 1000 Sunshine Lane, Austin, Texas 78701, or place of employment of Mother at State of Texas, 1111 Worker's Lane, Austin, TX 78701 for any purpose, except to exercise visitation granted in this decree.

4. **Interfering in any way with the Mother's possession of the children or taking or retaining possession of the children, directly or in concert with other persons, except as permitted by order of the Court.**

5. **Coming within 200 yards of, entering, or remaining on the premises of the children's day-care facility, Little Guys School, 1000 Munchkin Lane, Austin, TX 78701; school, Best Elementary School, 1111 Learn Alot Lane, Austin, TX 78701; or other day-care facility or school about which Father receives written notice, except as permitted in this court order.**

Father cannot be present within 200 yards, except as specifically stated in this order (i.e., drop-off, pickup).

Service of Writ

Petitioner and Respondent waive issuance and service of the writ of injunction, by stipulation or as evidenced by the signatures below. IT IS ORDERED that Petitioner and Respondent shall be deemed to be duly served with the writ of injunction.

Change of Petitioner's Name

IT IS ORDERED AND DECREED that Mother's name is changed to Single Mother.

Court Costs

IT IS ORDERED AND DECREED that costs of court are to be borne by the party who incurred them.

Resolution of Temporary Orders

IT IS ORDERED AND DECREED that Petitioner and Respondent are discharged from all further liabilities and obligations imposed by the temporary order of this Court rendered on November 1, 2009.

Discharge from Discovery Retention Requirement

IT IS ORDERED AND DECREED that the parties and their respective attorneys are discharged from the requirement of keeping and storing the documents produced in this case in accordance with rule 191.4(d) of the Texas Rules of Civil Procedure.

Clarifying Orders

Without affecting the finality of this Final Decree of Divorce, this Court expressly reserves the right to make orders necessary to clarify and enforce this decree.

Relief Not Granted

IT IS ORDERED AND DECREED that all relief requested in this case and not expressly granted is denied. This is a final judgment, for which let execution and all writs and processes necessary to enforce this judgment issue. This judgment finally disposes of all claims and all parties and is appealable.

Date of Judgment

This divorce judicially PRONOUNCED AND RENDERED in court at Austin, Travis County, Texas, on January 25, 2010 and further noted on the court's docket sheet on the same date, but signed on March 1, 2010.

____
JUDGE PRESIDING

APPROVED AS TO FORM ONLY:
Smart Attorney's Firm
1000 Legal Lane
Austin, TX 78705
Tel: (512) 222-2222
Fax: (512) 333-3333

By:____
Smart Attorney
Attorney for Petitioner
State Bar No. 11111111

Attorney contact info

Smart Lawyer's Firm
1000 Brief Street
Austin, TX 78701
Tel: (512) 777-7777
Fax: (512) 888-8888

By:____
Smart Lawyer
Attorney for Respondent
State Bar No. 222222222

NO. D-1-FM-09-000001

IN THE INTEREST OF	§	**IN THE DISTRICT COURT**
	§	
CHILD	§	**98TH JUDICIAL DISTRICT**
	§	
A CHILD	§	**TRAVIS COUNTY, TEXAS**

FINAL PROTECTIVE ORDER

On December 15, 2009 the Court heard the Application of Mother for a Protective Order.

Appearances

Applicant, Mother, appeared in person and through attorney of record, Great Attorney, and announced ready.

Respondent, Father, appeared in person and through attorney of record, Fantastic Attorney, and announced ready.

Jurisdiction

The Court, after examining the record and hearing the evidence and argument of counsel, finds that all necessary prerequisites of the law have been satisfied and that this Court has jurisdiction over the parties and subject matter of this case.

Findings

The Court finds that Applicant is Respondent's spouse.

The Court finds that family violence has occurred and that family violence is likely to occur in the future. The Court finds that Respondent, Father, has committed family violence. The Court finds that the following protective orders are for the safety and welfare and in the best interest of members of the family and are necessary for the prevention of family violence.

Orders

1

IT IS ORDERED that Respondent, Father, is:

Prohibited from committing family violence, as defined by section 71.004 of the Texas Family Code.

Prohibited from communicating directly with Child in a threatening or harassing manner.

Prohibited from communicating a threat through any person to Child.

Prohibited from engaging in conduct directed specifically toward Child, including following Child, that is reasonably likely to harass, annoy, alarm, abuse, torment, or embarrass Child.

Prohibited from going to or near the residences, child-care facilities, or schools Child normally attends or in which Child normally resides. Specifically, Respondent is prohibited from going to or near Child's school or Extend-a-Care and specifically must maintain a distance of 200 yards from those places.

Prohibited from removing Child from the possession of Mother.

Prohibited from transferring, encumbering, or otherwise disposing of property mutually owned or leased by the parties, except when in the ordinary course of business.

Prohibited from possessing a firearm or ammunition, unless Respondent is a peace officer, as defined by section 1.07 of the Texas Penal Code, actively engaged in employment as a sworn, full-time paid employee of a state agency or political subdivision.

IT IS ORDERED that the license to carry a concealed handgun that was issued to Respondent, Father, under section 411.177 of the Texas Government Code is suspended.

IT IS ORDERED that Applicant, Mother, is granted exclusive possession of the residence located at 123 Happy Ln., Austin, TX 78701.

2

IT IS ORDERED that Respondent complete a program that has begun the accreditation process under article 42.141 of the Texas Code of Criminal Procedure.

IT IS FURTHER ORDERED that Respondent file with the Court, before the sixtieth day after the date this order is rendered, an affidavit stating either that Respondent has started the program or that the program is not available within a reasonable distance of Respondent's residence. IT IS FURTHER ORDERED that, if Respondent files an affidavit that Respondent has started the program, Respondent shall file with the Court before the date this protective order expires (1) a statement that Respondent completed the program not later than the earlier of the thirtieth day before this protective order expires or the thirtieth day before the first anniversary of the date of this protective order is issued and (2) a letter, notice, or certificate from the program that verifies Respondent's completion of the program. If Respondent fails to provide the affidavit and, if required, the statement and verification of completion of the program as ordered, Respondent may be punished for contempt of court, as provided by section 21.002 of the Texas Government Code, by a fine not to exceed $500, by confinement in jail for a term not to exceed six months, or by both.

IT IS ORDERED that Applicant, Mother, is awarded exclusive use and possession of the following property:

2004 Ford Escort.

IT IS ORDERED that Respondent, Father, is granted possession of and access to Child as follows: On the first third and fifth Fridays of each month beginning at 6:00 p.m. and ending the following Sunday at 6:00 p.m. IT IS FURTHER ORDERED that Applicant shall have possession of the child at all times not specifically granted to Respondent in this order.

3

NOTICE TO ANY PEACE OFFICER OF THE STATE OF TEXAS: YOU MAY USE REASONABLE EFFORTS TO ENFORCE THE TERMS OF CHILD CUSTODY SPECIFIED IN THIS ORDER. A PEACE OFFICER WHO RELIES ON THE TERMS OF A COURT ORDER AND THE OFFICER'S AGENCY ARE ENTITLED TO THE APPLICABLE IMMUNITY AGAINST ANY CLAIM, CIVIL OR OTHERWISE, REGARDING THE OFFICER'S GOOD FAITH ACTS PERFORMED IN THE SCOPE OF THE OFFICER'S DUTIES IN ENFORCING THE TERMS OF THE ORDER THAT RELATE TO CHILD CUSTODY. ANY PERSON WHO KNOWINGLY PRESENTS FOR ENFORCEMENT AN ORDER THAT IS INVALID OR NO LONGER IN EFFECT COMMITS AN OFFENSE THAT MAY BE PUNISHABLE BY CONFINEMENT IN JAIL FOR AS LONG AS TWO YEARS AND A FINE OF AS MUCH AS $10,000.

IT IS ORDERED that Father pay to Mother for the support of Child $500 per month, with the first payment being due and payable on January 1, 2010 and a like payment being due and payable on the first day of each month thereafter until further order of this Court. IT IS ORDERED that all payments shall be made through the State Child Support Disbursement Unit, P.O. Box 11111, San Antonion, TX 78751 and then remitted by that agency to Mother for the support of the child.

IT IS ORDERED that Respondent, Father, vacate the residence located at 123 Happy Ln., Austin, TX 78701, by 5:00 p.m. on December 16, 2009.

IT IS FURTHER ORDERED that the sheriff of Travis County, Texas, is ORDERED to provide a law enforcement officer from their department to accompany Applicant, Mother, to the residence at 123 Happy Ln., Austin, TX 78701, to inform Respondent that the Court has

4

ordered Respondent excluded from the residence, to protect Applicant while Applicant takes possession of the residence and Respondent takes possession of Respondent's necessary and personal property, and, if Respondent refuses to vacate the residence, to remove Respondent from the residence and arrest Respondent for violating the Court's order.

Attorney's Fees

The Court finds that Father should be assessed $2,000 as attorney's fees for the services of Great Attorney. IT IS ORDERED that Great Attorney is awarded judgment of $2,000 for legal services rendered. The judgment, for which let execution issue, is awarded against Father.

Fees, Charges, and Expenses

IT IS ORDERED that Father shall pay the $16 protective order fee, the standard fee for cost of service of this order, the costs of court, and all other fees, charges, or expenses incurred in connection with this order.

IT IS THEREFORE ORDERED that Respondent shall pay $16.00 to the clerk of this Court on or before the sixtieth day after the date this order is rendered at the Travis County District Clerk's Office, 1000 Guadalupe, Austin, TX 78701 by cash, cashier's check, or money order.

Relief Not Granted

IT IS ORDERED that all relief requested in the Application for Protective Order but not expressly granted is denied.

Order Forwarded

A copy of this order, along with the information provided by Applicant's attorney that is required under section 411.042(b)(6) of the Texas Government Code, shall be forwarded by the clerk of this Court to the sheriff and the appropriate constable of Travis County, Texas. A copy of this order shall be forwarded by the clerk of this Court to Child's School, Child's Extend-a-Care Program..

Effective Period

This order shall continue in full force and effect until December 15, 2011.

Warnings:

A PERSON WHO VIOLATES THIS ORDER MAY BE PUNISHED FOR CONTEMPT OF COURT BY A FINE OF AS MUCH AS $500 OR BY CONFINEMENT IN JAIL FOR AS LONG AS SIX MONTHS, OR BOTH.

NO PERSON, INCLUDING A PERSON WHO IS PROTECTED BY THIS ORDER, MAY GIVE PERMISSION TO ANYONE TO IGNORE OR VIOLATE ANY PROVISION OF THIS ORDER. DURING THE TIME IN WHICH THIS ORDER IS VALID, EVERY PROVISION OF THIS ORDER IS IN FULL FORCE AND EFFECT UNLESS A COURT CHANGES THE ORDER.

IT IS UNLAWFUL FOR ANY PERSON, OTHER THAN A PEACE OFFICER, AS DEFINED BY SECTION 1.07, PENAL CODE, ACTIVELY ENGAGED IN EMPLOYMENT AS A SWORN, FULL-TIME PAID EMPLOYEE OF A STATE AGENCY OR POLITICAL SUBDIVISION, WHO IS SUBJECT TO A PROTECTIVE ORDER TO POSSESS A FIREARM OR AMMUNITION.

A VIOLATION OF THIS ORDER BY COMMISSION OF AN ACT PROHIBITED BY THE ORDER MAY BE PUNISHABLE BY A FINE OF AS MUCH AS $4,000 OR BY CONFINEMENT IN JAIL FOR AS LONG AS ONE YEAR, OR BOTH. AN ACT THAT

RESULTS IN FAMILY VIOLENCE MAY BE PROSECUTED AS A SEPARATE MISDEMEANOR OR FELONY OFFENSE. IF THE ACT IS PROSECUTED AS A SEPARATE FELONY OFFENSE, IT IS PUNISHABLE BY CONFINEMENT IN PRISON FOR AT LEAST TWO YEARS.

POSSESSION OF A FIREARM WHILE THIS PROTECTIVE ORDER IS IN EFFECT MAY SUBJECT RESPONDENT TO FEDERAL CRIMINAL PENALTIES.

IT IS UNLAWFUL FOR ANY PERSON WHO IS SUBJECT TO A PROTECTIVE ORDER TO KNOWINGLY PURCHASE, RENT, LEASE, OR RECEIVE AS A LOAN OR GIFT FROM ANOTHER, A HANDGUN FOR THE DURATION OF THIS ORDER.

INTERSTATE VIOLATION OF THIS PROTECTIVE ORDER MAY SUBJECT RESPONDENT TO FEDERAL CRIMINAL PENALTIES. THIS PROTECTIVE ORDER IS ENFORCEABLE IN ALL FIFTY STATES, THE DISTRICT OF COLUMBIA, TRIBAL LANDS, AND U.S. TERRITORIES.

SIGNED on ________________________.

____

JUDGE PRESIDING

Information about Respondent to Aid Law Enforcement Officers:

Name: Father
Home address: 123 Bluebird Ln., Austin, Travis County, Texas 78701
Home telephone number: 512-444-4444
Work address: 123 Work Hard Ln., Austin, Travis County, TX 78701
Work telephone number: 512-555-5555
Date of birth: 01/01/1978
Color of eyes: blue
Color of hair: brown

7

Height: 5'11"
Weight: 195
Sex: Male
Race: White
Personal Descriptors: Teardrop tattoo below right eye.
Social Security number: XXX-XX-X889
Driver's license or identification number and issuing state: Texas; DL#11111111

APPROVED AS TO FORM ONLY:

Great Attorney's Law Firm
1111 Litigation Lane
Austin, TX 78701
Tel: (512) 111-1111
Fax: (512) 222-2222

By: ______________________________
Great Attorney
Attorney for Applicant
State Bar No.: 11111111

Fantastic Attorney's Law Firm
222 Brief Street
Austin, TX 78701
Phone: (512) 333-3333
Fax: (512) 444-4444

By: ______________________________
Fantastic Attorney
Attorney for Respondent
State Bar No.: 22222222

8

THIS IS ONLY A SAMPLE POA.
You may be shown a different one.

POWER OF ATTORNEY
CARE AND CUSTODY OF CHILD OR CHILDREN

POAs may grant very specific or very broad authority, or something in between.

KNOW ALL PERSONS BY THESE PRESENTS: That the undersigned,

____, parent of the child identified
(printed name of parent)

below, residing at ____
(address with city, state)

or any location within any state of the United States of America, hereby make,

constitute and appoint: ____, as
(printed name of Attorney-in-Fact)

This one seems to grant very broad authority, including broad education and health care decisions.

the true and lawful Attorney-in-Fact of the undersigned, to act in name, place and stead of the undersigned, to do and execute all or any of the following acts, deeds and things with respect to the care and custody of the following child:

____
(printed name of child)

1. To participate in decisions regarding the child's education, including attending conferences with the child's teachers or any other educational authorities, granting permission for the child's participation in school trips and other activities, and making any other decisions and reviewing and executing any documents pertinent to the child's education.

Broad education authority

2. To grant permission and consent to the child participating in any activity sponsored by any group, association or organization which activity the Attorney-in-Fact may deem appropriate.

3. To make health care decisions on behalf of the child, including making decisions regarding the medical or dental care, whether routine or emergency in nature; including admissions to hospitals or other institutions; to consent to, to refuse to consent to, or withdraw consent to the provision of any care, tests, treatment, surgery, or procedure to maintain, diagnose or treat a physical or mental condition, as well as the right to sign such

Health care

POWER OF ATTORNEY
PAGE 1

medical forms as may be necessary to carry out such decisions; to talk with health care personnel who may be treating the child, and to examine the child's medical records and to consent to the disclosure of such records in circumstances the Attorney-in-Fact may deem appropriate; to file claims for medical insurance and to obtain information from any insurance company with respect to any policy of health or medical insurance under which the child may be insured; provided however that the Attorney-in-Fact shall not be required to execute any documents which would involve incurring any personal liability for such treatment and care, and the undersigned affirms that the undersigned will be responsible for payment for any such care or treatment consented to by the Attorney-in-Fact of the undersigned which is not covered by insurance.

4. To generally do and perform all matters and things, to execute all other instruments of every kind which may be necessary or proper to effectuate all powers hereinabove specifically granted, with the same full powers and to all intents and purposes, with the same validity as the undersigned could, if personally present; and hereby ratifying and confirming whatsoever said Attorney-in-Fact of the undersigned shall and may do, by virtue hereto.

5. Specifically excluded from the authority and powers granted herein is the authority or power to consent to marriage or adoption of the child named herein.

The POA is good only within this time period.

It may be revoked before the written deadline.

The powers herein granted to said Attorney-in-Fact of the undersigned shall be exercisable by any one or all of them and from time to time from ______________________ (date), until ______________________ (date).

This power of Attorney shall remain in full force and effect until the date stated above, and any party dealing with the Attorney-in-Fact during such time shall be fully protected and is hereby discharged, released and indemnified from so doing in respect of any matter relating hereto unless such particular

POWER OF ATTORNEY
PAGE 2

____
Signature/Relationship to child

____
City, County, State of Residence

STATE OF TEXAS

COUNTY OF

BEFORE ME, the undersigned notary public, on this day personally appeared ____, known to me to be the person whose name is subscribed above, and, having been by me duly sworn, on his/her oath states and deposes as follows: "I am of sound mind and otherwise capable of understanding and executing this document."
Further, affiant sayeth not.

____
(printed name of notary)

____
(signed name of notary)

SUBSCRIBED AND SWORN TO BEFORE ME, on this __________ day of _________________________, 2010 to certify which witness my hand and seal of office.

Notary Public, State of Texas
My Commission expires: _______________

POWER OF ATTORNEY
PAGE 3

Notes

Chapter 1. Terminology in Court Orders

1. Tex. Fam. Code Sec. 153.073.
2. Tex. Fam. Code Sec. 153.074.
3. Tex. Fam. Code Sec. 153.132.
4. For the code sections dealing with standard possession, see Tex. Fam. Code Secs. 153.312 et seq.
5. There are two SPOs: one for parents who live within 100 miles of each other, and another for parents who live over 100 miles from each other. The primary difference between these SPOs is summer possession and spring break possession.
6. Holiday possession supersedes the weekend schedule. Tex. Fam. Code Sec. 153.314.
7. See Tex. Fam. Code Sec. 153.002.
8. For the full protective order statute, see Tex. Fam. Code Secs. 71.001 et seq., also known as Title 4 of the Texas Family Code.
9. See Tex. Fam. Code Sec. 85.025(a).
10. See Tex. Fam. Code Sec. 85.025(c).
11. See Tex. Fam. Code Secs. 6.501 et seq. and 105.001.
12. See Tex. Fam. Code Sec. 161.103.
13. See Tex. Fam. Code Sec. 161.001.
14. See Tex. Fam. Code Sec. 161.206.
15. For more information about guardianships, see Tex. Prob. Code Chap. 13.
16. For more information about powers of attorney, see Tex. Prob. Code Chap. 12.

Chapter 2. Who Is a Parent?

1. Tex. Fam. Code Sec. 101.024.
2. Tex. Fam. Code Sec. 160.201(a).
3. Tex. Fam. Code Sec. 160.201, 160.204.
4. Tex. Educ. Code Sec. 26.002. Emphasis added.
5. The term "parental relation" has been used in Texas education law as far back as 1917, in the context of truancy cases (*Odam v. State*, 81 Tex.Crim. 204, 194 S.W. 829 (1917). Yet it has never been defined by Texas courts or the Texas attorney general. Even today Texas Education Code Section 25.0951 describes a school district's duty to file a complaint or referral with a court against a student's parent or "a person standing in parental relation" for a student's failure to attend school. We think this term extends only to the primary caregiver of a student in the absence of a biological or adoptive parent. One Texas attorney general's opinion encountering this term in a truancy case wearily says, "For the sake of brevity, we will hereinafter refer to a 'parent or person standing in parental relation' as simply a 'parent'" (Tex. Atty. Gen. Op. LO-94-058 1994). Other jurisdictions have reached the conclusion that a nonparent may stand "in parental relation" to a child when the nonparent (1) assumes the obligations incident to parental status, even without legally adopting the child, and (2) voluntarily performs the parental duties to generally provide for the child—e.g., *Smith v. Smith*, 922 So.2d 94 (Ala. 2005); *Logan v. Logan*, 730 So.2d 1124, 1126 (Miss. 1998); *Hamilton v. Foster*, 260 Neb. 887, 903–04, 620 N.W.2d 103, 116 (2000); *Fevig v. Fevig*, 90 N.M. 51, 53, 559 P.2d 839, 841 (1977); *Rutkowski v. Wasko*, 286 A.D. 327, 331, 143 N.Y.S.2d 1, 5 (1955).
6. There are at least two situations when schools may not have an adult with whom to deal on behalf of a minor student: (1) when the student is 17—or is at least 16 and living apart from the minor's parents, managing conservator, or guardian—and the student is managing his or her own financial affairs and has petitioned a court for removal of the disabilities of a minor (Tex. Family Code Sec. 31.001); and (2) in the case of an unaccompanied homeless youth under the McKinney-Vento Homeless Assistance Act, 42 United States Code Sec. 11431.
7. Tex. Educ. Code Sec. 25.001(j).
8. Tex. Educ. Code Sec. 26.002.
9. See 20 United States Code Secs. 1415(b)(2), 1439(a)(5), and 1401(23).
10. See 34 C.F.R. Sec. 99.3.
11. Educators have the right to use reasonable force on a student in order to control, train, and educate the child (Tex. Penal Code Sec. 9.62). This has been commonly construed to apply to protecting the child's health, safety,

and welfare and to maintaining order in a group. It may also apply to corporal punishment, if the school district allows it by policy. (Even if allowed, however, we dissuade educators from using corporal punishment. It provides fertile ground for accusations of misconduct, including assault, abuse, or neglect, and exposes the administrator to potential liability. It doesn't seem worth it. For interesting legal analyses and other legal references on an educator's right to administer corporal punishment, see Tex. Atty. Gen. Op. GA-0374 [2005] and Tex. Atty. Gen. Op. GA-0202 [2004].)

12. Tex. Fam. Code 34.002(a). See that subsection for a complete list of acts that a parent can delegate to a relative.

13. See *Byrd v. Livingston ISD*, 674 F.Supp. 225, 43 Ed. Law Rep. 583 (E.D.Tex. 1987).

14. Also see Tex. Educ. Code Sec. 25.001(b)(9): "The board of trustees of a school district or its designee shall admit into the public schools of the district free of tuition a person who is over five and younger than 21 years of age on the first day of September of the school year in which admission is sought, and may admit a person who is at least 21 years of age and under 26 years of age for the purpose of completing the requirements for a high school diploma, if: . . . the person does not reside in the school district *but the grandparent of the person: (A) resides in the school district; and (B) provides a substantial amount of after-school care for the person as determined by the board.*"

15. Notwithstanding Tex. Educ. Code Sec. 25.001(b)(9), a parent's rights will trump any other person's rights, absent a court order to the contrary.

16. Tex. Fam. Code 151.001(a)(10).

Chapter 3. What Are the Basic Parental Rights in Education?

1. Sec. 9101(32), ESEA.
2. Tex. Educ. Code Sec. 26.001(e).
3. Tex. Educ. Code Sec. 26.003(a)(2). Emphasis added.
4. Tex. Educ. Code Sec. 26.003(a)(3).
5. Tex. Educ. Code Sec. 26.003(b).
6. Tex. Educ. Code Sections 26.005, 26.006.
7. Per Tex. Educ. Code Sec. 26.009(a)(2) and 26.009(b), an employee is not required to obtain consent if the videotape or voice recording is to be used only for (1) safety purposes, including the maintenance of order and discipline in common areas of the school or on school buses; (2) a purpose related to a cocurricular or extracurricular activity; (3) a purpose related to regular classroom instruction; or (4) media coverage of the school..
8. Tex. Educ. Code Sec. 21.057.
9. Tex. Educ. Code Sec. 26.010.
10. Tex. Educ. Code Sec. 26.008, 26.0081.
11. Tex. Educ. Code Sec. 26.0091.
12. Tex. Educ. Code Sec. 26.007.
13. Tex. Educ. Code Sec. 26.001(d). Also see school board policy FNG (local).
14. Tex. Fam. Code Sec. 151.001.
15. Tex. Fam. Code Sec. 151.001(a)(10).
16. Tex. Fam. Code Sec. 151.001(a)(3).
17. 20 United States Code Sec. 1415.
18. See *Lopez v. Metropolitan Gov't of Nashville*, ____ F.Supp. 2d ____, 2009 WL1971452 (M.D.Tenn. 2009).
19. *Rodgers v. Duncanville ISD,* 2005 WL 770712 (N.D.Tex. 2005). This parent pulled his child out of the Duncanville ISD and enrolled him in the Dallas ISD. Undeterred, he then sued the Dallas ISD for basically the same reasons and was ordered to pay a $500 fine for bringing another frivolous lawsuit against school officials. *Rodgers v. Dallas ISD,* 2007 WL 1686508 (N.D.Tex. 2007).
20. Tex. Educ. Code Sec. 37.124(c)(1). Also see school board policy GKA (legal).

Chapter 4. Parental Right Changes by a Court or a Legal Document

1. See Tex. Fam. Code Sec. 151.001.
2. Tex. Fam. Code Sec. 151.001(3), 151.001(10).
3. Tex. Educ. Code Sec. 26.002.
4. See Tex. Fam. Code Secs. 161.103 and 161.001.
5. Tex. Fam. Code Sec. 161.206(b).
6. To be reminded about the meaning of the term "joint managing conservator," look back at chapter 1.
7. See Tex. Fam. Code Sec. 153.071.
8. See Tex. Fam. Code Chap. 156.
9. See Tex. Fam. Code Secs. 71.0021, 71.003–71.006, 81.001, and 85.001.
10. Tex. Fam. Code Sec. 85.025.
11. Ibid.
12. See Tex. Fam. Code Sec. 85.021(3).
13. See Tex. Fam. Code Secs. 85.021–85.022.
14. Tex. Fam. Code Sec. 82.002(c).
15. Tex. Fam. Code Sec. 85.042.
16. See Tex. Fam. Code Sec. 85.026.
17. Tex. Penal Code Sec. 25.07.
18. Tex. Code Crim. Proc. Art. 14.03(b).
19. Tex. Penal Code Sec. 25.07(e).

20. See pages 36–38 of the divorce decree in appendix B.

21. See Tex. Prob. Code Chap. 13.

22. It should be noted that a school administrator should never suggest that someone file for guardianship so that the person can enroll a child in a particular school. A court may not grant guardianship sought for the primary purpose of enabling the minor to establish residency for enrollment in a certain school or district. Tex. Prob. Code Sec. 684(b)(3).

23. See Tex. Prob. Code Chap. 12.

24. In 2011 the law was amended to include agreements between a parent and a person with whom the child is placed under a parental child safety placement agreement. Tex. Fam. Code Sec. 34.001.

25. Tex. Fam. Code Sec. 34.002(a). This subsection presents a complete list of acts that a parent can delegate to a relative.

26. Tex. Fam. Code Sec. 34.002(b).

27. Tex. Fam. Code Secs. 34.003–34.005. Section 34.003 describes the required contents for an authorization agreement for nonparent relative:

Sec. 34.003. CONTENTS OF AUTHORIZATION AGREEMENT.

(a) The authorization agreement must contain:

(1) the following information from the relative of the child to whom the parent is giving authorization:

(A) the name and signature of the relative;

(B) the relative's relationship to the child; and

(C) the relative's current physical address and telephone number or the best way to contact the relative;

(2) the following information from the parent:

(A) the name and signature of the parent; and

(B) the parent's current address and telephone number or the best way to contact the parent;

(3) the information in Subdivision (2) with respect to the other parent, if applicable;

(4) a statement that the relative has been given authorization to perform the functions listed in Section 34.002(a) as a result of a voluntary action of the parent and that the relative has voluntarily assumed the responsibility of performing those functions;

(5) statements that neither the parent nor the relative has knowledge that a parent, guardian, custodian, licensed child-placing agency, or other authorized agency asserts any claim or authority inconsistent with the authorization agreement under this chapter with regard to actual physical possession or care, custody, or control of the child;

(6) statements that:

(A) to the best of the parent's and relative's knowledge:

(i) there is no court order or pending suit affecting the parent-child relationship concerning the child;

(ii) there is no pending litigation in any court concerning:

(a) custody, possession, or placement of the child; or

(b) access to or visitation with the child; and

(iii) the court does not have continuing jurisdiction concerning the child; or

(B) the court with continuing jurisdiction concerning the child has given written approval for the execution of the authorization agreement accompanied by the following information:

(i) the county in which the court is located;

(ii) the number of the court; and

(iii) the cause number in which the order was issued or the litigation is pending;

(7) a statement that to the best of the parent's and relative's knowledge there is no current, valid authorization agreement regarding the child;

(8) a statement that the authorization is made in conformance with this chapter;

(9) a statement that the parent and the relative understand that each party to the authorization agreement is required by law to immediately provide to each other party information regarding any change in the party's address or contact information;

(10) a statement by the parent that establishes the circumstances under which the authorization agreement expires, including that the authorization agreement:

(A) is valid until revoked;

(B) continues in effect after the death or during any incapacity of the parent; or

(C) expires on a date stated in the authorization agreement; and

(11) space for the signature and seal of a notary public.

(b) The authorization agreement must contain the following warnings and disclosures:

(1) that the authorization agreement is an important legal document;

(2) that the parent and the relative must read all of the warnings and disclosures before signing the authorization agreement;

(3) that the persons signing the authorization agreement are not required to consult an attorney but are advised to do so;

(4) that the parent's rights as a parent may be adversely affected by placing or leaving the parent's child with another person;

(5) that the authorization agreement does not confer on the relative the rights of a managing or possessory conservator or legal guardian;

(6) that a parent who is a party to the authorization

agreement may terminate the authorization agreement and resume custody, possession, care, and control of the child on demand and that at any time the parent may request the return of the child;

(7) that failure by the relative to return the child to the parent immediately on request may have criminal and civil consequences;

(8) that, under other applicable law, the relative may be liable for certain expenses relating to the child in the relative's care but that the parent still retains the parental obligation to support the child;

(9) that, in certain circumstances, the authorization agreement may not be entered into without written permission of the court;

(10) that the authorization agreement may be terminated by certain court orders affecting the child;

(11) that the authorization agreement does not supersede, invalidate, or terminate any prior authorization agreement regarding the child;

(12) that the authorization agreement is void if a prior authorization agreement regarding the child is in effect and has not expired or been terminated;

(13) that, except as provided by Section 34.005(a-1), the authorization agreement is void unless:

(A) the parties mail a copy of the authorization agreement by certified mail, return receipt requested, or international registered mail, return receipt requested, as applicable, to a parent who was not a party to the authorization agreement, if the parent is living and the parent's parental rights have not been terminated, not later than the 10th day after the date the authorization agreement is signed; and

(B) if the parties do not receive a response from the parent who is not a party to the authorization agreement before the 20th day after the date the copy of the authorization agreement is mailed under Paragraph (A), the parties mail a second copy of the authorization agreement by first class mail or international first class mail, as applicable, to the parent not later than the 45th day after the date the authorization agreement is signed; and

(14) that the authorization agreement does not confer on a relative of the child the right to authorize the performance of an abortion on the child or the administration of emergency contraception to the child.

28. Tex. Fam. Code Sec. 34.007(a).
29. Tex. Fam. Code Sec. 34.007(b).
30. Tex. Fam. Code Sec. 34.004.
31. Tex. Fam. Code Sec. 34.008(a).
32. Tex. Fam. Code Secs. 34.004(b) and 34.008(b).
33. Tex. Fam. Code Sec. 34.008(d).
34. Tex. Fam. Code Sec. 34.008(c).

Chapter 5. Parental Rights at School

1. *Doe v. Covington County Sch. Dist.*, 649 F.3d 335, 340 (5th Cir. 2011), *reversed*, 675 F.3d 849 (5th Cir. 2012) (en banc).

2. Ibid. at 341.

3. *Doe v. Covington County Sch. Dist.*, 649 F.3d 335, 340 (5th Cir. 2011), *reversed*, 675 F.3d 849 (5th Cir. 2012) (en banc).

4. *Doe v. Covington County Sch. Dist.*, 675 F.3d 849 (5th Cir. 2012) (en banc).

5. Tex. Penal Code 25.07.

6. See appendix C for an example of a protective order prohibiting a father from coming within 200 yards of his child's school. You will notice in the example order that the name and address of the child's school are omitted. Texas law specifically provides that even if this information is omitted, the PO is still criminally enforceable. Typically, the omission of the school location is allowed because the perpetrator of domestic violence does not know the location, and the person requesting the PO wants to keep it that way.

7. See chapter 9 on reporting abuse and neglect, and see Tex. Fam. Code Sec. 261.001 for the definitions of "abuse" and "neglect."

8. Tex. Fam. Code Chap. 42.

9. Tex. Fam. Code Sec. 42.003.

10. Tex. Educ. Code Sec. 22.0511.

11. See *In re J.S.P.*, 278 S.W.3d 414, 417 (Tex. App.—San Antonio, 2008).

12. The one exception is if there is a protective order prohibiting Parent A from being at the school. As discussed in chapters 2 and 4, parents may not consent to the violation of a protective order.

Chapter 6. Parental Right to Make Educational Decisions

1. Sometimes in this situation, the court will name a "tiebreaker" (i.e., a person who will get to make the ultimate decision if the parents cannot reach an agreement). This person may be the teacher, the school counselor, the child's therapist, or someone else altogether. If the order names someone, and the parents cannot reach an agreement, ask the appointed person to weigh in on the matter.

2. But note Tex. Educ. Code Sec. 26.002, which

specifies that a person who is not entitled to possession of or access to a child under a court order is not a "parent" for the purposes of the Texas Education Code. It is our belief that a court order specific to the rights and duties of a particular parent supersedes this generalization in the Texas Education Code.

3. In a situation where there is a SAPCR order giving a parent the right to make educational decisions and a subsequent protective order prohibiting contact between the parent and a child, it is usual for the parent obtaining the protective order to go back to court to modify the SAPCR order. The educational rights can be modified so that the parent found to have committed violence no longer has the right to make educational decisions. However, unless this modification is made, the right to make educational decisions remains as set out in the SAPCR order.

4. See Tex. Educ. Code Sec. 26.002.

5. Ibid.

6. See ibid.

Chapter 7. Parental Right to School Records

1. Tex. Educ. Code Sec. 26.004.

2. Tex. Fam. Code Sec. 153.073.

3. A very helpful FAQ section that describes and explains FERPA regulations, including the 2008 amendments, may be found at http://edocket.access.gpo.gov/cfr_2009/julqtr/pdf/34cfr99.3.pdf.

4. 34 C.F.R. Sec. 99.31(a)(1).

5. 34 C.F.R. Sec. 99.31 (a)(1)(ii).

6. . www2.ed.gov/policy/gen/guid/fpco/pdf/ht12-17-08-att.pdf, page 6 of comments.

7. 34 C.F.R. Sec. 99.11.

8. 34 C.F.R. Sec. 99.4.

9. 34 C.F.R. Sec. 99.20.

10. 34 C.F.R. Sec. 99.7.

11. 34 C.F.R. Sec. 99.10.

12. 34 C.F.R. Sec. 99.3.

13. 34 C.F.R. Sec. 99.32(a)(5).

14. Ibid.

15. Ibid. Among the December 2008 amendments is a regulation acknowledging the U.S. Supreme Court decision in *Owasso Indep. Sch. Dist. v. Falvo*, 534 U.S. 426 (2002). In this case a parent complained that confidentiality had been breached by the practice of peer grading in class. The parent was certainly on to something: this was a gray area of FERPA, brought about by a student's red pen. The case placed in jeopardy a classroom grading practice that extends back in our nation's history at least to the days of Laura Ingalls Wilder. The Supreme Court ruled in favor of the school, and this new regulation confirms the interpretation.

16. 34 C.F.R. Sec. 99.3.

17. Tex. Health & Safety Code Sec. 611.0045(b). In *Abrams v. Jones*, 35 S.W.3d 620 (Tex. 2000), the Texas Supreme Court held that "because subsection (b) [of section 611.0045] may limit a patient's rights to his or her own records, subsection (b) can also limit a parent's or third party's right to a patient's records when the third party or parent stands in the patient's stead." *Abrams*, at 626.

18. Tex. Atty. Gen. Op. JC-0538 (2002).

19. Tex. Fam. Code Sec. 32.004(b).

20. Andrea J. Sedlak, David Finkelhor, Heather Hammer, and Dana J. Schultz, U.S. Department of Justice, "National Estimates of Missing Children: An Overview," in *National Incidence Studies of Missing, Abducted, Runaway, and Thrownaway Children* (Washington, DC: Office of Juvenile Justice and Delinquency Prevention, Office of Justice Programs, U.S. Department of Justice, October 2002), 2.

21. The following articles of the Texas Code of Criminal Procedure apply:

Art. 63.019. SCHOOL RECORDS SYSTEM.

(a) On enrollment of a child under 11 years of age in a school for the first time at the school, the school shall:
  (1) request from the person enrolling the child the name of each previous school attended by the child;
  (2) request from each school identified in Subdivision (1), the school records for the child and, if the person enrolling the child provides copies of previous school records, request verification from the school of the child's name, address, birth date, and grades and dates attended; and
  (3) notify the person enrolling the student that not later than the 30th day after enrollment, or the 90th day if the child was not born in the United States, the person must provide:
    (A) a certified copy of the child's birth certificate; or
    (B) other reliable proof of the child's identity and age and a signed statement explaining the person's inability to produce a copy of the child's birth certificate.

(b) If a person enrolls a child under 11 years of age in school and does not provide the valid prior school information or documentation required by this section, the school shall notify the appropriate law enforcement agency before the 31st day after the person fails to comply with this section. On receipt of notification, the law enforcement agency shall immediately check the clearinghouse to determine if the child has been reported missing. If the child has been reported missing, the law enforcement agency shall immediately notify other appropriate law enforcement agencies that the missing child has been located.

Art. 63.020. DUTY OF SCHOOLS AND OTHER ENTITIES TO FLAG MISSING CHILDREN'S RECORDS.

(a) When a report that a child under 11 years of age is missing is received by a law enforcement agency, the agency shall immediately notify each school and day care facility that the child attended or in which the child was enrolled as well as the bureau of vital statistics, if the child was born in the state, that the child is missing.
(b) On receipt of notice that a child under 11 years of age is missing, the bureau of vital statistics shall notify the appropriate municipal or county birth certificate agency that the child is missing.
(c) A school, day care facility, or birth certificate agency that receives notice concerning a child under this section shall flag the child's records that are maintained by the school, facility, or agency.
(d) The law enforcement agency shall notify the clearinghouse that the notification required under this section has been made. The clearinghouse shall provide the notice required under this section if the clearinghouse determines that the notification has not been made by the law enforcement agency.
(e) If a missing child under 11 years of age, who was the subject of a missing child report made in this state, was born in or attended a school or licensed day care facility in another state, the law enforcement agency shall notify law enforcement or the missing and exploited children clearinghouse in each appropriate state regarding the missing child and request the law enforcement agency or clearinghouse to contact the state birth certificate agency and each school or licensed day care facility the missing child attended to flag the missing child's records.

22. The following article of the Texas Code of Criminal Procedure applies:

Art. 63.021. SYSTEM FOR FLAGGING RECORDS.
(a) On receipt of notification by a law enforcement agency or the clearinghouse regarding a missing child under 11 years of age, the school, day care facility, or birth certificate agency shall maintain the child's records in its possession so that on receipt of a request regarding the child, the school, day care facility, or agency will be able to notify law enforcement or the clearinghouse that a request for a flagged record has been made.
(b) When a request concerning a flagged record is made in person, the school, day care facility, or agency may not advise the requesting party that the request concerns a missing child and shall:
   (1) require the person requesting the flagged record to complete a form stating the person's name, address, telephone number, and relationship to the child for whom a request is made and the name, address, and birth date of the child;
   (2) obtain a copy of the requesting party's driver's license or other photographic identification, if possible;
   (3) if the request is for a birth certificate, inform the requesting party that a copy of a certificate will be sent by mail; and
   (4) immediately notify the appropriate law enforcement agency that a request has been made concerning a flagged record and include a physical description of the requesting party, the identity and address of the requesting party, and a copy of the requesting party's driver's license or other photographic identification.
(c) After providing the notification required under Subsection (a)(4), the school, day care facility, or agency shall mail a copy of the requested record to the requesting party on or after the 21st day after the date of the request.
(d) When a request concerning a flagged record is made in writing, the school, day care facility, or agency may not advise the party that the request concerns a missing child and shall immediately notify the appropriate law enforcement agency that a request has been made concerning a flagged record and provide to the law enforcement agency a copy of the written request. After providing the notification under this subsection, the school, day care facility, or agency shall mail a copy of the requested record to the requesting party on or after the 21st day after the date of the request.

Chapter 8. Reporting Child Abuse and Neglect

1. See Tex. Fam. Code Sec. 261.101(b).

2. See Tex. Fam. Code Sec. 261.109.

3. The law also requires the reporting of abuse, neglect, or exploitation of the elderly and the disabled (Tex. Hum. Res. Code Chap. 48).

4. *White v. State*, 50 S.W.3d 31 (Tex. App.—Waco 2001, pet. ref'd).

5. Tex. Fam. Code Sec. 261.001(1).

6. From the Texas Penal Code:

Sec. 21.02: CONTINUOUS SEXUAL ABUSE OF YOUNG CHILD OR CHILDREN.
(a) In this section, "child" has the meaning assigned by Section 22.011(c).
(b) A person commits an offense if:
   (1) during a period that is 30 or more days in duration, the person commits two or more acts of sexual abuse, regardless of whether the acts of sexual abuse are committed against one or more victims; and

(2) at the time of the commission of each of the acts of sexual abuse, the actor is 17 years of age or older and the victim is a child younger than 14 years of age.

(c) For purposes of this section, "act of sexual abuse" means any act that is a violation of one or more of the following penal laws:

(1) aggravated kidnapping under Section 20.04(a)(4), if the actor committed the offense with the intent to violate or abuse the victim sexually;

(2) indecency with a child under Section 21.11(a)(1), if the actor committed the offense in a manner other than by touching, including touching through clothing, the breast of a child;

(3) sexual assault under Section 22.011;

(4) aggravated sexual assault under Section 22.021;

(5) burglary under Section 30.02, if the offense is punishable under Subsection (d) of that section and the actor committed the offense with the intent to commit an offense listed in Subdivisions (1)–(4); and

(6) sexual performance by a child under Section 43.25.

***

(g) It is an affirmative defense to prosecution under this section that the actor:

(1) was not more than five years older than:

(A) the victim of the offense, if the offense is alleged to have been committed against only one victim; or

(B) the youngest victim of the offense, if the offense is alleged to have been committed against more than one victim;

(2) did not use duress, force, or a threat against a victim at the time of the commission of any of the acts of sexual abuse alleged as an element of the offense; and

(3) at the time of the commission of any of the acts of sexual abuse alleged as an element of the offense:

(A) was not required under Chapter 62, Code of Criminal Procedure, to register for life as a sex offender; or

(B) was not a person who under Chapter 62 had a reportable conviction or adjudication for an offense under this section or an act of sexual abuse as described by Subsection (c).

(h) An offense under this section is a felony of the first degree, punishable by imprisonment in the Texas Department of Criminal Justice for life, or for any term of not more than 99 years or less than 25 years.

7. From the Texas Penal Code:

Sec. 21.11. INDECENCY WITH A CHILD.

(a) A person commits an offense if, with a child younger than 17 years and not the person's spouse, whether the child is of the same or opposite sex, the person:

(1) engages in sexual contact with the child or causes the child to engage in sexual contact; or

(2) with intent to arouse or gratify the sexual desire of any person:

(A) exposes the person's anus or any part of the person's genitals, knowing the child is present; or

(B) causes the child to expose the child's anus or any part of the child's genitals.

8. From the Texas Penal Code:

Sec. 22.011. SEXUAL ASSAULT.

(a) A person commits an offense if the person:

(1) intentionally or knowingly:

(A) causes the penetration of the anus or sexual organ of another person by any means, without that person's consent;

(B) causes the penetration of the mouth of another person by the sexual organ of the actor, without that person's consent; or

(C) causes the sexual organ of another person, without that person's consent, to contact or penetrate the mouth, anus, or sexual organ of another person, including the actor; or

(2) intentionally or knowingly:

(A) causes the penetration of the anus or sexual organ of a child by any means;

(B) causes the penetration of the mouth of a child by the sexual organ of the actor;

(C) causes the sexual organ of a child to contact or penetrate the mouth, anus, or sexual organ of another person, including the actor;

(D) causes the anus of a child to contact the mouth, anus, or sexual organ of another person, including the actor; or

(E) causes the mouth of a child to contact the anus or sexual organ of another person, including the actor.

(b) A sexual assault under Subsection (a)(1) is without the consent of the other person if:

(1) the actor compels the other person to submit or participate by the use of physical force or violence;

(2) the actor compels the other person to submit or participate by threatening to use force or violence against the other person, and the other person believes that the actor has the present ability to execute the threat;

(3) the other person has not consented and the actor knows the other person is unconscious or physically unable to resist;

(4) the actor knows that as a result of mental disease or defect the other person is at the time of the sexual assault incapable either of appraising the nature of the act or of resisting it;

(5) the other person has not consented and the actor knows the other person is unaware that the sexual assault is occurring;

(6) the actor has intentionally impaired the other person's power to appraise or control the other person's conduct by administering any substance without the other person's knowledge;
(7) the actor compels the other person to submit or participate by threatening to use force or violence against any person, and the other person believes that the actor has the ability to execute the threat;
(8) the actor is a public servant who coerces the other person to submit or participate;
(9) the actor is a mental health services provider or a health care services provider who causes the other person, who is a patient or former patient of the actor, to submit or participate by exploiting the other person's emotional dependency on the actor;
(10) the actor is a clergyman who causes the other person to submit or participate by exploiting the other person's emotional dependency on the clergyman in the clergyman's professional character as spiritual adviser; or
(11) the actor is an employee of a facility where the other person is a resident, unless the employee and resident are formally or informally married to each other under Chapter 2, Family Code.

(c) In this section:
(1) "Child" means a person younger than 17 years of age who is not the spouse of the actor. . . .

(d) It is a defense to prosecution under Subsection (a)(2) that the conduct consisted of medical care for the child and did not include any contact between the anus or sexual organ of the child and the mouth, anus, or sexual organ of the actor or a third party.

(e) It is an affirmative defense to prosecution under Subsection (a)(2) that:
(1) the actor was not more than three years older than the victim and at the time of the offense:
(A) was not required under Chapter 62, Code of Criminal Procedure, to register for life as a sex offender; or
(B) was not a person who under Chapter 62, Code of Criminal Procedure, had a reportable conviction or adjudication for an offense under this section; and
(2) the victim:
(A) was a child of 14 years of age or older; and
(B) was not a person whom the actor was prohibited from marrying or purporting to marry or with whom the actor was prohibited from living under the appearance of being married under Section 25.01.

9. "Sexual conduct" includes deviant sexual intercourse, sexual contact, and sexual intercourse.

10. Tex. Fam. Code Sec. 261.001(4).

11. 40 Tex. Admin. Code Sec. 700.403.

12. 40 Tex. Admin. Code Sec. 700.501(11).

13. Tex. Fam. Code Sec. 261.101(b) (emphasis added).

14. Tex. Fam. Code Sec. 261.301(c).

15. 40 Tex. Admin. Code Sec. 700.404.

16. The exact response or level of discipline will vary depending on the circumstances. Immediate parental notification is almost always a good first step (unless that might further jeopardize a student's safety or health). Consult your supervisor and school lawyer and policy FFH for guidance.

17. Tex. Fam. Code Sec. 261.101(a).

18. A lawyer must make a report to the authorities even if the lawyer learns that his or her client is the abuser or the one responsible for neglect. However, a lawyer may not be made to testify against his or her client in any later criminal proceeding (Tex. Fam. Code Sec. 261.202).

19. Ibid.

20. Tex. Family Code Sec. 261.101(b).

21. See *Guthrie v. Texas Dept. of Protective and Regulatory Services*, WL 298741 (Tex. App.—Austin 2001, unpublished), which states: "The trial of this case involved more than thirty witnesses, including the Guthries; their friends, neighbors and family; employees of Child Protective Services ('CPS') and affiliated service providers; peace officers and *school bus drivers*; and various others" (emphasis added).

22. Tex. Fam. Code Sec. 261.110.

23. Tex. Fam. Code Sec. 261.110(m).

24. Tex. Fam. Code Sec. 261.109.

25. See Tex. Penal Code Sec. 12.21.

26. *Matthews v. Winona Indep. Sch. Dist.*, Dkt. No. 010-R2-1002 (Tex. Comm'r Educ. 2002).

27. *Perry v. S.N.*, 973 S.W.2d 301 (Tex. 1998).

28. *Doe v. S&S Consol. Indep. Sch. Dist.*, 149 F.Supp.2d 591, 594 (W.D. Tex. 2002), *affirmed*, 309 F.3d 307 (5th Cir. 2002).

29. *Doe v. Rains Indep. Sch. Dist.*, 865 F.Supp. 375 (E.D. Tex. 1994), *reversed*, 66 F.3d 1402 (5th Cir. 1995).

30. *Doe v. Taylor Indep. Sch. Dist.*, 15 F.3d 443 (5th Cir. 1994).

31. Tex. Fam. Code Sec. 261.102.

32. *White v. State.*

33. Tex. Fam. Code Sec. 261.103.

34. Tex. Fam. Code Sec. 261.101.

35. Tex. Fam. Code Sec. 261.201(g).

36. Tex. Fam. Code Sec. 261.106.

37. Tex. Fam. Code Sec. 261.108.

38. Tex. Fam. Code Sec. 153.013.

39. 40 Tex. Admin Code Sec. 700.407.

40. 40 Tex. Admin Code Sec. 700.408.

41. Tex. Fam. Code Sec. 261.401(b); 40 Tex. Admin. Code Sec. 700.411.

42. Tex. Admin. Code Sec. 700.409(a).

43. Tex. Admin. Code Sec. 700.409.

44. 40 Tex. Admin. Code Sec. 700.508(b).

45. Tex. Fam. Code Sec. 261.401(b).

46. 40 Tex. Admin. Code Sec. 700.516. See also Tex. Fam. Code Sec. 261.309.

Chapter 9. Help! I've Been Subpoenaed!

1. The person serving the subpoena might not be "official-looking." Although sheriffs and constables serve subpoenas, lawyers, more often than not, hire private process servers to serve subpoenas. They are usually faster and more persistent. The only qualification in the court rules is that the process server be over 18 years old and not a party to the lawsuit. See Tex. R. Civ. Proc. Sec. 176.5 for who can serve a subpoena and the Tex. Civ. Prac. & Rem. Code Sec. 22.001 for information about the required witness fees.

2. Tex. R. Civ. Proc. Sec. 176.6 states: "A person served with a subpoena must comply with the command stated therein unless discharged by the court or by the party summoning such witness. A person commanded to appear and give testimony must remain at the place of deposition, hearing, or trial from day to day until discharged by the court or by the party summoning the witness."

3. Tex. Labor Code Sec. 52.051. An employer who interferes with the employee's right to comply with a subpoena may be held in contempt by the court. An employee penalized by the employer may be entitled to damages. A school district may have a policy requiring an employee to reimburse the district for any for any fees obtained by an employee for activities such as performing jury duty and serving as a subpoenaed witness.

4. *Reagan v. Guardian Life Ins. Co.*, 166 S.W.2d 909 (Tex. 1942); *James v. Brown*, 637 S.W.2d 914 (Tex. 1982).

5. This question is probably objectionable since it is the fact finder's job (the judge or jury's job) to decide this question after hearing the evidence.

6. Tex. R. Civ. Proc. Sec. 176.7 states: "A party causing a subpoena to issue must take reasonable steps to avoid imposing undue burden or expense on the person served. In ruling on objections or motions for protection, the court must provide a person served with a subpoena an adequate time for compliance, protection from disclosure of privileged material or information, and protection from undue burden or expense. The court may impose reasonable conditions on compliance with a subpoena, including compensating the witness for undue hardship."

7. *Hatteberg v. Hatteberg*, 933 S.W.2d 522, 526 (Tex. App.—Houston [1st Dist.] 1994, no writ)—9 days not diligent; *Victor M. Solis Underground Util. & Paving Co. v. City of Laredo*, 751 S.W.2d 532, 537 (Tex. App.—San Antonio 1988, writ denied)—3 days not diligent; *Dairyland Cty. Mut. Ins. Co. v. Keys*, 568 S.W.2d 457, 460 (Tex. App.—Tyler 1978, writ ref'd n.r.e.)—day of trial not diligent.

8. Tex. R. Civ. Proc. 176.5(a).

9. Tex. Civ. Prac. & Rem. Code 22.001(a); Tex. Atty. Gen. Op. DM-342 (1995). These sections provide that, regardless of whether the subpoena requires attendance in a courthouse or other setting, the $10 fee applies.

10. Tex. R. Civ. Proc. 176.3.

11. There is a provision for a litigant to have subpoenas served for free by the constable's office if the party can show an inability to pay.

12. A "friendly witness" is one who seems willing to come to court and is not anticipated to say anything negative about the party calling the witness to testify.

13. Tex. R. Civ. Proc. Sec. 176.8 states: "Failure by any person without adequate excuse to obey a subpoena served upon that person may be deemed a contempt of the court from which the subpoena is issued or a district court in the county in which the subpoena is served, and may be punished by fine or confinement, or both."

14. The order requiring law enforcement to pick up the AWOL witness is called a writ of attachment. See *In re Z.A.T.*, 193 S.W.3d 197, 207 (Tex. App.—Waco 2006, pet. denied).

15. If the child is seeing the school's counselor, see chapter 7 for information about whether these records must be revealed.

16. In most cases the attorneys will invoke "the Rule." This refers to Rule 614 of the Texas Rules of Evidence, but lawyers and judges just refer to it as "the Rule." This means that while the trial is going on, witnesses will be required to stay out of the courtroom until after they testify. The witnesses may not talk to the other witnesses or the parties in the case. Witnesses may speak only to the lawyers. Chatting about the case with the parties or other witnesses while you are waiting to testify may cause you to be reprimanded by the court and/or you may not be allowed to testify.

17. This is the single-most difficult task for any witness to achieve. It is a quintessential example of something easier said than done. Some witnesses are incapable of

doing it—describing how to make a clock, when asked only for the time. Here is our brief attempt to put you on the path to brevity. Assume you are asked: "Isn't it true you got your hair cut on Wednesday?" If you got your haircut on Thursday, then the answer to the question is no. If your answer is, "No, I was going to get my haircut on Wednesday, but I overslept, so I got it cut on Thursday," then you have answered more than was asked. While this is a silly example, you get the picture. No one is great at this, and you will catch yourself answering more than was asked. Don't sweat it. Do your best and move on.

About the Authors

Since 1989, **Kevin Lungwitz** has represented Texas school employees. In March 2007 he began Lungwitz Law Firm (LungwitzLaw.com) to focus on Texas educator representation and the delivery of educator seminars and workshops. His peers in the practice of Texas school law elected him to serve as chair of the School Law Section of the State Bar in 2006–2007. Since 2007 Kevin has served as the outside general counsel for the Texas Elementary Principals and Supervisors Association, advising hundreds of TEPSA members and writing a regular legal column in the organization's newsletter, *TEPSA News.* He continues to represent a variety of Texas administrators and teachers. Prior to opening the law firm, Kevin served for more than 16 years as general counsel and staff attorney for the Texas State Teachers Association. Over the years, he has represented hundreds of school employees in school board meetings, TEA and SBEC hearings, and CPS investigations and at trial and appeal, including several educator cases before the Texas Supreme Court. Kevin makes numerous presentations every year to school employees, lawyers, and education students on public education issues.

Jeana Lungwitz has been the clinical professor in the Domestic Violence Clinic at the University of Texas School of Law since 1997 when she cofounded the clinic with attorney Sarah Buel. In that capacity, Jeana is regularly in the Travis County Courthouse representing parties in family law matters, and teaching law students the practice of law. In 2003 the Texas Supreme Court appointed her to the Supreme Court Protective Order Task Force. Jeana has received many awards for her legal service through the years, including the Pathfinders Award, presented by the Travis County Women Lawyers' Association (2010); the Regina Rogoff Award for Public Service, presented by the Austin Bar Association (2009); the Texas Law Fellows Excellence in Public Interest Award (2008 and 1996); and the Travis County Women Lawyers' Association Public Interest Law Award (1999). She is also a coshareholder in The Lungwitz Law Firm, P.C. with her husband, Kevin, where she makes frequent presentations on school law issues.

Kevin and Jeana graduated from the Texas Tech University School of Law in 1989, where they met. They were both licensed to practice law in Texas that same year. Jeana and Kevin are very involved in raising two lovely daughters and have each served as PTA officers, booster club officers, and members of numerous committees in their daughters' public schools. They have never once disagreed about their daughters' education in the presence of a teacher or administrator.